Learn TensorFlow 2.0

Implement Machine Learning and Deep Learning Models with Python

Pramod Singh
Avinash Manure

Apress®

Learn TensorFlow 2.0: Implement Machine Learning and Deep Learning Models with Python

Pramod Singh
Bangalore, Karnataka, India

Avinash Manure
Bangalore, India

ISBN-13 (pbk): 978-1-4842-5560-5
https://doi.org/10.1007/978-1-4842-5558-2

ISBN-13 (electronic): 978-1-4842-5558-2

Managing Director, Apress Media LLC: Welmoed Spahr
Acquisitions Editor: Celestin Suresh John
Development Editor: James Markham
Coordinating Editor: Aditee Mirashi

Cover designed by eStudioCalamar

Cover image designed by Freepik (www.freepik.com)

Distributed to the book trade worldwide by Springer Science+Business Media New York, 233 Spring Street, 6th Floor, New York, NY 10013. Phone 1-800-SPRINGER, fax (201) 348-4505, e-mail orders-ny@springer-sbm.com, or visit www.springeronline.com. Apress Media, LLC is a California LLC, and the sole member (owner) is Springer Science+Business Media Finance Inc (SSBM Finance Inc). SSBM Finance Inc is a **Delaware** corporation.

For information on translations, please e-mail rights@apress.com, or visit www.apress.com/rights-permissions.

Apress titles may be purchased in bulk for academic, corporate, or promotional use. eBook versions and licenses are also available for most titles. For more information, reference our Print and eBook Bulk Sales web page at www.apress.com/bulk-sales.

Any source code or other supplementary material referenced by the authors in this book is available to readers on GitHub, via the book's product page, located at www.apress.com/978-1-4842-5560-5. For more detailed information, please visit www.apress.com/source-code.

Printed on acid-free paper

I dedicate this book to my wife, Neha, my son, Ziaan, and my parents. Without you, this book wouldn't have been possible. You complete my world and are the source of my strength.

—Pramod Singh

I dedicate this book to my wife, Jaya, for constantly encouraging me to do the best in whatever I undertake, and also my mom and dad, for their unconditional love and support, which have made me what I am today. Last but not least, my thanks to Pramod, for trusting me and giving me the opportunity to coauthor this book.

—Avinash Manure

Table of Contents

About the Authors

Pramod Singh is currently employed as a machine learning expert at Walmart Labs. He has extensive hands-on experience in machine learning, deep learning, artificial intelligence (AI), data engineering, designing algorithms, and application development. He has spent more than ten years working on multiple data projects at different organizations. He's the author of three books: *Machine Learning with PySpark, Learn PySpark,* and *Learn TensorFlow 2.0*. He is also a regular speaker at major tech conferences, such as O'Reilly Strata Data and AI Conferences. Pramod holds a BTech in electrical engineering from Mumbai University and an MBA from Symbiosis University. He also holds data science certification from IIM–Calcutta. Pramod lives in Bangalore, India, with his wife and three-year-old son. In his spare time, he enjoys playing guitar, coding, reading, and watching football.

Avinash Manure is a senior data scientist at Publicis Sapient with more than eight years of experience using data to solve real-world business challenges. He is proficient in deploying complex machine learning and statistical modeling algorithms/techniques to identify patterns and extract valuable insights for key stakeholders and organizational leadership.

Avinash holds a bachelor's degree in electronics engineering from Mumbai University and holds an MBA in marketing from the University of Pune. He and his wife are currently settled in Bangalore. He enjoys traveling to new places and reading motivational books.

About the Technical Reviewer

 **Jojo Moolayil** is an AI professional and author of three books on machine learning, deep learning, and the Internet of Things (IoT). He is currently working as a research scientist—AI at Amazon Web Services, in their Vancouver, British Columbia, office.

Jojo was born and raised in Pune, India, and graduated from the University of Pune with a major in information technology engineering. His passion for problem solving and data-driven decision making led him to start a career with Mu Sigma Inc., the world's largest pure-play analytics provider. There, he was responsible for developing machine learning and decision science solutions to complex problems for major health care and telecom companies. He later worked with Flutura (an IoT analytics startup) and General Electric, with a focus on industrial AI, in Bangalore.

In his current role with Amazon, he works on researching and developing large-scale AI solutions to combat fraud and enrich the customers' payment experience in the cloud. Jojo is also actively involved as a tech reviewer and AI consultant to leading publishers and has reviewed more than a dozen books on machine learning, deep learning, and business analytics.

You can reach Jojo at the following:

- www.jojomoolayil.com/
- www.linkedin.com/in/jojo62000
- twitter.com/jojo62000

Acknowledgments

This is my third book with Apress, and a lot of thought went into writing it. The main objective was to introduce to the IT community the critical changes introduced in the new version of TensorFlow. I hope readers will find it useful, but first, I'd like to thank a few people who helped me along the journey. First, I must thank the most important person in my life, my beloved wife, Neha, who selflessly supported me throughout and sacrificed so much to ensure that I completed this book.

I must also thank my coauthor, Avinash Manure, who expended a great amount of effort to complete the project on time. In addition, my thanks to Celestin Suresh John, who believed in me and offered me this opportunity to write another book for Apress. Aditee Mirashi is one of the best editors in India. This is my third book with her, and it was quite exciting to collaborate again. She was, as usual, extremely supportive and always available to accommodate my requests. To James Markham, who had the patience to review every line of code and check the appropriateness of each example, thank you for your feedback and your encouragement. It really made a difference to me and the book. I also want to thank my mentors who have constantly encouraged me to chase my dreams. Thank you Sebastian Keupers, Dr. Vijay Agneeswaran, Sreenivas Venkatraman, Shoaib Ahmed, and Abhishek Kumar.

Finally, I am infinitely grateful to my son, Ziaan, and my parents, for the endless love and support, irrespective of circumstances. You all make my world beautiful.

—Pramod Singh

ACKNOWLEDGMENTS

This is my first book, and a very special one indeed. As mentioned by Pramod, the objective of this book is to introduce readers to TensorFlow 2.0 and explain how this platform has evolved over the years to become one of the most popular and user-friendly source libraries for machine learning currently available. I would like to thank Pramod for having confidence in me and giving me the golden opportunity to coauthor this book. As this is my first book, Pramod has been guiding and helping me to complete it.

I would like to thank my wife, Jaya, who made sure I had the right environment at home to concentrate and complete this book on time. I would also like to thank the publishing team—Aditee Mirashi, Matthew Moodie, and James Markham—who have helped me immensely in ensuring that this book reaches the audience in its best state. I would also like to thank my mentors, who made sure I grew professionally and personally by always supporting me in my dreams and guiding me toward them. Thank you Tristan Bishop, Erling Amundson, Deepak Jain, Dr. Vijay Agneeswaran, and Abhishek Kumar for all the support that you have extended to me. Last but not least, I would like to acknowledge my parents, my friends, and colleagues, who have always been there in my tough times and motivated me to follow my dreams.

—Avinash Manure

Introduction

Google has been a pioneer in introducing groundbreaking technology and products. TensorFlow is no exception, when it comes to efficiency and scale, yet there have been some adoption challenges that have convinced Google's TensorFlow team to implement changes to facilitate ease of use. Therefore, the idea of writing this book was simply to introduce to readers these important changes made by the TensorFlow core team. This book focuses on different aspects of TensorFlow, in terms of machine learning, and goes deeper into the internals of the recent changes in approach. This book is a good reference point for those who seek to migrate to TensorFlow to perform machine learning.

This book is divided into three sections. The first offers an introduction to data processing using TensorFlow 2.0. The second section discusses using TensorFlow 2.0 to build machine learning and deep learning models. It also includes neuro-linguistic programming (NLP) using TensorFlow 2.0. The third section covers saving and deploying TensorFlow 2.0 models in production. This book also is useful for data analysts and data engineers, as it covers the steps of big data processing using TensorFlow 2.0. Readers who want to transition to the data science and machine learning fields will also find that this book provides a practical introduction that can lead to more complicated aspects later. The case studies and examples given in the book make it really easy to follow and understand the relevant fundamental concepts. Moreover, there are very few books available on TensorFlow 2.0, and this book will certainly increase the readers' knowledge. The strength of this book lies in its simplicity and the applied machine learning to meaningful data sets.

We have tried our best to inject our entire experience and knowledge into this book and feel it is specifically relevant to what businesses are seeking to solve real challenges. We hope you gain some useful takeaways from it.

CHAPTER 1

Introduction to TensorFlow 2.0

The intent of this book is to introduce readers to the latest version of the TensorFlow library. Therefore, this first chapter focuses mainly on what has changed in the TensorFlow library since its first version, TensorFlow 1.0. We will cover the various changes, in addition to highlighting the specific parts for which changes are yet to be introduced. This chapter is divided into three sections: the first discusses the internals of TensorFlow; the second focuses on the changes that have been implemented in TensorFlow 2.0 after TensorFlow 1.0; and the final section covers TensorFlow 2.0 installation methods and basic operations.

You may already be aware that TensorFlow is widely used as a machine learning implementation library. It was created by Google as part of the Google Brain project and was later made available as an open source product, as there were multiple machine learning and deep learning frameworks that were capturing the attention of users. With open source availability, more and more people in the artificial intelligence (AI) and machine learning communities were able to adopt TensorFlow and build features and products on top of it. It not only helped users with implementation of standard machine learning and deep learning algorithms but also allowed them to implement customized and differentiated versions of algorithms for business applications and

© Pramod Singh, Avinash Manure 2020
P. Singh and A. Manure, *Learn TensorFlow 2.0*,
https://doi.org/10.1007/978-1-4842-5558-2_1

various research purposes. In fact, it soon became one of the most popular libraries in the machine learning and AI communities—so much so that people have been building a huge number of apps using TensorFlow under the hood. This is principally owing to the fact that Google itself uses TensorFlow in most of its products, whether Google Maps, Gmail, or other apps.

While TensorFlow had its strengths in certain areas, it also had a few limitations, owing to which developers found it a bit difficult to adopt, compared to such other libraries as PyTorch, Theano, and OpenCV. As Google's TensorFlow team took the feedback of the TensorFlow community seriously, it went back to the drawing board and started working on most of the changes required to make TensorFlow even more effective and easy to work with, soon launching the TensorFlow 2.0 alpha version this year. TensorFlow 2.0 claims to have removed some of the previous hurdles, in order to allow developers to use TensorFlow even more seamlessly. In this chapter, we will go over those changes one by one, but before covering these, let us spend some time understanding what exactly TensorFlow is and what makes it one of the best available options to perform machine learning and deep learning today.

Tensor + Flow = TensorFlow

Tensors are the building blocks of TensorFlow, as all computations are done using tensors. So, what exactly is a tensor?

According to the definition provided by Google's TensorFlow team,

A tensor is a generalization of vectors and matrices to potentially higher dimensions. Internally, TensorFlow represents tensors as n-dimensional arrays of base datatypes.

But we would like to delve a little deeper into tensors, in order to provide more than a general overview of what they are. We would like to compare them with vectors or matrices, so as to highlight the key dynamic property that makes tensors so powerful. Let us start with a simple vector. A vector is commonly understood as something that has a magnitude and a direction. Simply put, it is an array that contains an ordered list of values. Without the direction of a vector, a tensor becomes a scalar value that has only magnitude.

A vector can be used to represent n number of things. It can represent area and different attributes, among other things. But let's move beyond just magnitude and direction and try to understand the real components of a vector.

Components and Basis Vectors

Let's suppose we have a vector $\hat{A}$, as shown in Figure 1-1. This is currently represented without any coordinate system consideration, but most of us are already aware of the Cartesian coordinate system (x, y, z axis).

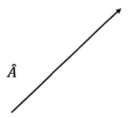

$\hat{A}$

Figure 1-1. *Simple vector*

If the vector $\hat{A}$ is represented in a three-dimensional space, it will look something like what is shown in Figure 1-2. This vector $\hat{A}$ can also be represented with the help of basis vectors.

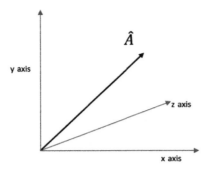

Figure 1-2. *Types of variables*

Basis vectors are associated with the coordinate system and can be used to represent any vector. These basis vectors have a length of 1 and, hence, are also known as *unit vectors.* The direction of these basis vectors is determined by their respective coordinates. For example, for three-dimensional representation, we have three basis vectors $(\hat{x}, \hat{y}, \hat{z})$, so $\hat{x}$ would have the direction of the x axis coordinate, and the $\hat{y}$ basis vector would have the direction of the y axis. Similarly, this would be the case for $\hat{z}$.

Once the basis vectors are present, we can use the coordinate system to find the components that represent the original vector $\hat{A}$. For simplicity, and to understand the components of the vector well, let's reduce the coordinate system from three dimensions to two. So, now the vector $\hat{A}$ looks something like what is shown in Figure 1-3.

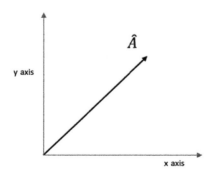

Figure 1-3. *2-dimensional view*

To find the first component of the vector $\hat{A}$ along the x axis, we will project it onto the x axis, as shown in Figure 1-4. Now, wherever the projection meets the x axis is known as the x component, or first component, of the vector.

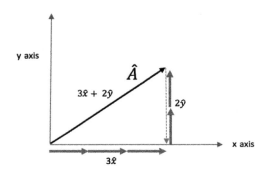

Figure 1-4. *Vector Magnitude*

If you look carefully, you can easily recognize this x component as the sum of a few basis vectors along the x axis. In this case, adding three basis vectors will give the x component of vector $\hat{A}$. Similarly, we can find the y component of vector $\hat{A}$ by projecting it on the y axis and adding up the basis vectors $(2\hat{y})$ along the y axis to represent it. In simple terms, we can think of this as how much one has to move in the x axis direction and y axis direction in order to reach vector $\hat{A}$.

$$\hat{A} = 3\hat{x} + 2\hat{y}$$

One other thing worth noting is that as the angle between vector $\hat{A}$ and the x axis increases, the x component decreases, but the y component increases. Vectors are part of a bigger class of objects known as tensors.

If we end up multiplying a vector with another vector, we get a result that is a scalar quantity, whereas if we multiply a vector with a scalar value, it just increases or decreases in the same proportion, in terms of its magnitude, without changing its direction. However, if we multiply

5

a vector with a tensor, it will result in a new vector that has a changed magnitude as well as a new direction.

Tensor

At the end of the day, a tensor is also a mathematical entity with which to represent different properties, similar to a scalar, vector, or matrix. It is true that a tensor is a generalization of a scalar or vector. In short, tensors are multidimensional arrays that have some dynamic properties. A vector is a one-dimensional tensor, whereas two-dimensional tensors are matrices (Figure 1-5).

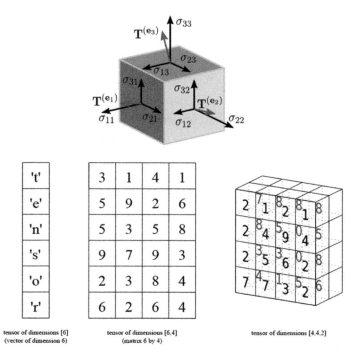

Figure 1-5. *Tensors*

Tensors can be of two types: constant or variable.

Rank

Ranking tensors can sometimes be confusing for some people, but in terms of tensors, rank simply indicates the number of directions required to describe the properties of an object, meaning the dimensions of the array contained in the tensor itself. Breaking this down for different objects, a scalar doesn't have any direction and, hence, automatically becomes a rank 0 tensor, whereas a vector, which can be described using only one direction, becomes a first rank tensor. The next object, which is a matrix, requires two directions to describe it and becomes a second rank tensor.

Shape

The shape of a tensor represents the number of values in each dimension.

> Scalar—32: The shape of the tensor would be [ ].

> Vector—[3, 4, 5]: The shape of the first rank tensor would be [3].

$$\text{Matrix} = \begin{matrix} 1 & 2 & 3 \\ 4 & 5 & 6 \\ 7 & 8 & 9 \end{matrix} : \text{The second rank tensor would}$$

> have a shape of [3, 3].

Flow

Now comes the second part of TensorFlow: flow. This is basically an underlying graph computation framework that uses tensors for its execution. A typical graph consists of two entities: nodes and edges, as shown in Figure 1-6. Nodes are also called vertices.

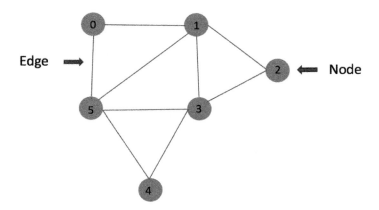

Figure 1-6. *Typical graph*

The edges are essentially the connections between the nodes/vertices through which the data flows, and nodes are where actual computation takes place. Now, in general, the graph can be cyclic or acyclic, but in TensorFlow, it is always acyclic. It cannot start and end at the same node. Let's consider a simple computational graph, as shown in Figure 1-7, and explore some of its attributes.

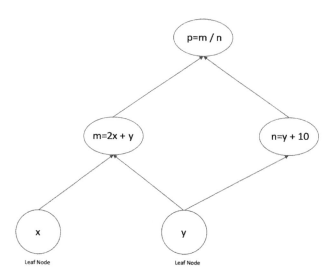

Figure 1-7. *Computational graph*

The nodes in the graph indicate some sort of computation, such as addition, multiplication, division, etc., except for the leaf nodes, which contain the actual tensors with either constant or variable values to be operated upon. These tensors flow through the edges or connections between nodes, and the computation at the next node results in formation of a new tensor. So, in the sample graph, a new tensor m is created through a computation at the node using other tensors x and y. The thing to focus on in this graph is that computations take place only at the next stage after leaf nodes, as leaf nodes can only be simple tensors, which become input for next-node computation flowing through edges. We can also represent the computations at each node through a hierarchical structure. The nodes at the same level can be executed in parallel, as there is no interdependency between them. In this case, m and n can be calculated in parallel at the same time. This attribute of graph helps to execute computational graphs in a distributed manner, which allows TensorFlow to be used for large-scale applications.

TensorFlow 1.0 vs. TensorFlow 2.0

Although TensorFlow was well adopted by the IT community after it was made available on an open source basis, there were still a lot of gaps, in terms of its user-friendliness. Users found it somewhat difficult to write TensorFlow-based code. Therefore, there was a lot of critical feedback by the developer and research communities regarding a few aspects of TensorFlow. As a result, the TensorFlow core development team started incorporating the suggested changes, to make the product easier to use and more effective. This section reviews those changes that have been incorporated into the TensorFlow 2.0 beta version. There are mainly three broad categories of changes that have been introduced in TensorFlow 2.0.

1. Usability-related modifications

2. Performance-related modifications

3. Deployment-related modifications

In this chapter, we are going to focus on only the first two categories, as Chapter 6 covers TensorFlow model deployment.

Usability-Related Changes

The first category of changes mainly focused on TensorFlow's ease of use and more consistent APIs. To go through these changes in detail, we have further subcategorized them according to three broad types.

1. Simpler APIs

2. Improved documentation

3. More inbuilt data sources

Simpler APIs

One of the most common criticisms of TensorFlow by users regarded its APIs, which were not user-friendly, thus a major focus of TensorFlow 2.0 has been on overhauling its APIs. Now, TensorFlow 2.0 provides two levels of APIs:

1. High-level APIs

2. Lower-level APIs

High-Level APIs

The high-level APIs make it easier to use TensorFlow for various applications, as these APIs are more intuitive in nature. These new high-level APIs have made debugging relatively easier than in earlier versions. As TensorFlow 1.0 was graph control–based, users were not able to debug their programs easily. TensorFlow 2.0 has now introduced eager execution, which performs operations and returns output instantly.

Lower-Level APIs

Another available set of APIs are lower level APIs which offer much more flexibility and configuration capability to the users in order to define and parameterise the models as per their specific requirements.

Session Execution

Readers who have used earlier versions of TensorFlow must have gone through the conventional procedure, session execution, to get to an operational graph, which likely consisted of the following steps:

1. First, create the `tf.Graph` object and set it to the default graph for the current scope.

2. Declare the computation part in TensorFlow: `c=tf.matmul(m,n)`.

3. Define the variable sharing and scope, as required.

4. Create and configure the `tf.Session` to build the graph and connect to the `tf.Session`.

5. Initialize all the variables in advance.

6. Use the `tf.Session.run` method to start the computation.

7. The `tf.Session.run` then triggers a procedure to compute the final output.

Eager Execution

With eager execution, TensorFlow 2.0 adopts a radically different approach and removes the need to execute most of the preceding steps.

1. TensorFlow 2.0 doesn't require the graph definition.

2. TensorFlow 2.0 doesn't require the session execution.

3. TensorFlow 2.0 doesn't make it mandatory to initialize variables.

4. TensorFlow 2.0 doesn't require variable sharing via scopes.

To understand these differences in detail, let's consider an example using TensorFlow 1.0 vs. TensorFlow 2.0.

```
[In]: import tensorflow as tf
[In]: tfs=tf.InteractiveSession()
[In]: c1=tf.constant(10,name='x')
[In]: print(c1)
[Out]: Tensor("x:0", shape=(), dtype=int32)
[In]: tfs.run(c1)
[Out]: 10
```

Import the new version of TensorFlow.

```
[In]: ! pip install -q tensorflow==2.0.0-beta1
[In]: import tensorflow as tf
[In]: print(tf.__version__)
[Out]: 2.0.0-beta1
[In]: c_1=tf.constant(10)
[In]: print(c_1)
[Out]: tf.Tensor(10, shape=(), dtype=int32)

# Operations
```

TensorFlow 1.0

```
[In]: c2=tf.constant(5.0,name='y')
[In]: c3=tf.constant(7.0,tf.float32,name='z')
[In]: op1=tf.add(c2,c3)
[In]: op2=tf.multiply(c2,c3)
[In]: tfs.run(op2)
[Out]: 35.0
[In]: tfs.run(op1)
[Out]: 12.0
```

TensorFlow 2.0

```
[In]:c2= tf.constant(5.0)
[In]:c3= tf.constant(7.0)
[In]: op_1=tf.add(c2,c3)
[In]: print(op_1)
[Out]: tf.Tensor(12.0, shape=(), dtype=float32)
[In]: op_2=tf.multiply(c2,c3)
[In]: print(op_2)
[Out]: tf.Tensor(35.0, shape=(), dtype=float32)
```

TensorFlow 1.0

```
g = tf.Graph()
with g.as_default():
    a = tf.constant([[10,10],[11.,1.]])
    x = tf.constant([[1.,0.],[0.,1.]])
    b = tf.Variable(12.)
    y = tf.matmul(a, x) + b
    init_op = tf.global_variables_initializer()

with tf.Session() as sess:
    sess.run(init_op)
    print(sess.run(y))
```

TensorFlow 2.0

```
a = tf.constant([[10,10],[11.,1.]])
x = tf.constant([[1.,0.],[0.,1.]])
b = tf.Variable(12.)
y = tf.matmul(a, x) + b
print(y.numpy())
```

Note   With TensorFlow 1.0 graph execution, the program state (such as variables) is stored in global collections, and their lifetime is managed by the `tf.Session` object. By contrast, during eager execution, the lifetime of state objects is determined by the lifetime of their corresponding Python object.

---

tf.function

Another powerful introduction of TensorFlow 2.0 is its `tf.function` capability, which converts relevant Python code into a formidable TensorFlow graph. It combines the flexibility of eager execution and strength of graph computations. As mentioned, TensorFlow 2.0 doesn't require the creation of a `tf.session` object. Instead, simple Python functions can be translated into a graph, using the `tf.function` decorator. In simple terms, in order to define a graph in TensorFlow 2.0, we must define a Python function and decorate it with `@tf.function`.

Keras

`tf.keras` was originally meant for small-scale models, as it had very simple APIs, but it was not scalable. TensorFlow also had introduced estimators that were designed for scaling and distributed training of machine learning models. Estimators had a huge advantage as they offered fault tolerance training in a distributed environment, but its APIs were not very user-friendly and were often regarded as confusing and a little hard to consume. With this in mind, TensorFlow 2.0 has introduced the standardized version of tf.keras, which combines the simplicity of Keras and power of estimators.

The code for tf.keras in TensorFlow versions 1.13 and 2.0 remain the same, but what has changed under the hood is the integration of Keras with new features of TensorFlow 2.0. To elaborate a little bit, if a particular piece of code was run with tf.keras in version 1.13, it would build a graph-based model that ran a session under the hood, which we initiated in the code. In version 2.0, the same model definition would run in eager mode, without any modification whatsoever.

With eager mode, it becomes easy to debug the code, compared to earlier graph-based execution. In eager mode, the data set pipelines behave exactly as those of a NumPy array, but TensorFlow takes care of the optimization in the best possible manner. Graphs are still very much part of TensorFlow but operate in the background.

Redundancy

Another useful feedback from the community regarding TensorFlow usage was that there were too many redundant components, which created confusion when using them in different places. For example, there were multiple optimizers and layers that one had to choose from while building the model. TensorFlow 2.0 has removed all the redundant elements and now comes with just one set of optimizers, metrics, losses, and layers. Duplicative classes have also been reduced, making it easier for users to figure out what to use and when.

Improved Documentation and More Inbuilt Data Sources

TensorFlow.org now contains much more exhaustive and detailed documentation for TensorFlow. This was critical from the user's perspective, as earlier versions had limited examples and tutorials for reference. This new documentation includes a lot of new data sources (small as well as big) for users to make use of in their programs or for learning purposes. The new APIs also make it very easy to import any new data source in TensorFlow. Some of the data sets from different domains that are made available within TensorFlow are shown in Table 1-1.

Table 1-1. *Data Sets Within TensorFlow 2.0*

Sr. No	Category	Data set
1	Text	`imdb_reviews`, `squad`
2	Image	`mnist`, `imagenet2012`, `coco2014`, `cifar10`
3	Video	`moving_mnist`, `starcraft_video`, `bair_robot_pushing_small`
4	Audio	`Nsynth`
5	Structured	`titanic`, `iris`

Performance-Related Changes

The TensorFlow development team also claims that new changes have improved product performance over earlier versions. Based on training and inference results using different processors (GPUs, TPUs), it seems TensorFlow has improved its speed two times, on average.

Installation and Basic Operations in TensorFlow 2.0

There are multiple ways in which we can use TensorFlow (local as well as cloud). In this section, we go over two ways in which TensorFlow 2.0 can be used locally as well as in the cloud.

1. Anaconda

2. Colab

3. Databricks

Anaconda

This is the simplest way of using TensorFlow on a local system. We can `pip` install the latest version of TensorFlow, as follows:

```
[In]: pip install -q tensorflow==2.0.0-beta1
```

Colab

The most convenient way to use TensorFlow, provided by Google's TensorFlow team, is Colab. Short for *Colaboratory*, this represents the idea of collaboration and online laboratories. It is a free Jupyter-based web environment requiring no setup, as it comes with all the dependencies prebuilt. It provides an easy and convenient way to let users write TensorFlow code within their browser, without having to worry about any sort of installations and dependencies. Let's go over the steps to see how to use Google Colab for TensorFlow 2.0.

1. Go to `https://colab.research.google.com`. You will see that the console has multiple options, as shown in Figure 1-8.

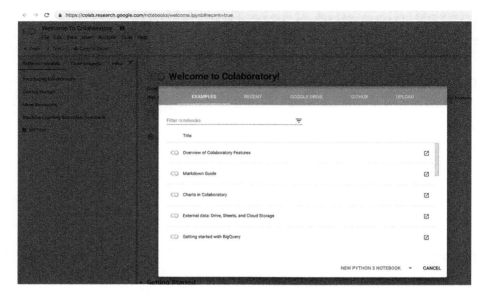

Figure 1-8. *Python Notebook Colaboratory (Colab) console*

2. Select the relevant option from the console, which
    contains the following five tabs:

    a. Examples. Shows the default notebooks provided in Colab

    b. Recent. The last few notebooks that the user worked on

    c. Google Drive. The notebooks linked to the user's Google
        Drive account

    d. GitHub. The option to link the notebooks present in the user's
        GitHub account

    e. Upload. The option to upload a new `ipynb` or `github` file

3. Click New Python 3 Notebook, and a new Colab
    notebook will appear, as shown in Figure 1-9.

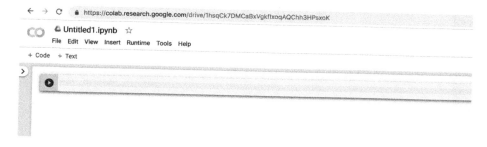

Figure 1-9. *New notebook*

    4.   Install and import TensorFlow 2.0 (Beta).

```
[In]:! pip install -q tensorflow==2.0.0-beta1
[In]: import tensorflow as tf
[In]: print(tf.__version__)
[Out]: 2.0.0-beta1
```

Another great advantage of using Colab is that it allows you to build your models on GPU in the back end, using Keras, TensorFlow, and PyTorch. It also provides 12GB RAM, with usage up to 12 hours.

Databricks

Another way to use TensorFlow is through the Databricks platform. The method of installing TensorFlow on Databricks is shown following, using a community edition account, but the same procedure can be adopted for business account usage as well. The first step is to log in to the Databricks account and spin up a cluster of desired size (Figures 1-10–1-12).

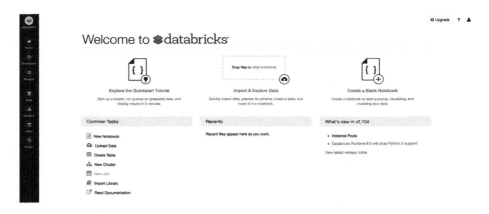

Figure 1-10. *Databricks*

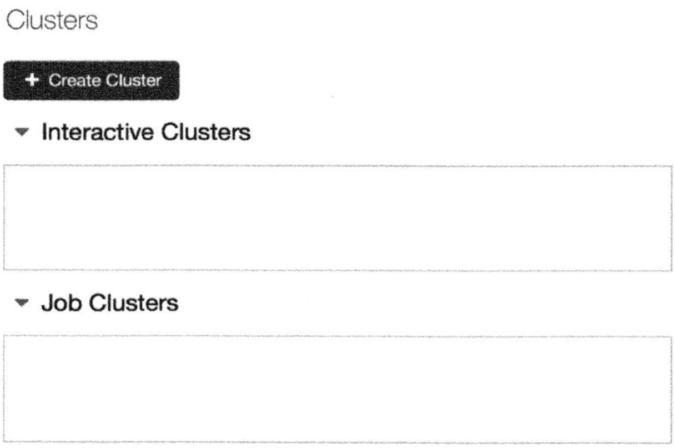

Clusters

+ Create Cluster

▾ **Interactive Clusters**

▾ **Job Clusters**

Figure 1-11. *Clusters*

Create Cluster

New Cluster   Cancel   Create Cluster   **0 Workers:** 0.0 GB Memory, 0 Cores, 0 DBU
1 **Driver:** 6.0 GB Memory, 0.88 Cores, 1 DBU ❷

Cluster Name

Tensorflow 2.0 Test

Databricks Runtime Version ❷

Runtime: 5.5 (Scala 2.11, Spark 2.4.3)

Python Version ❷

3

Instance

Free 6GB Memory: As a Community Edition user, your cluster will automatically terminate after an idle period of two hours.
For more configuration options, **please** upgrade your Databricks subscription.

Figure 1-12.   Cluster settings

Once the cluster is up and running, we go to the Libraries options of the cluster, via Actions, as shown in Figure 1-13.

Name	State	Nodes	Driver	Worker	Runtime
● Tensorflow 2.0 Test	Running	1 (0 spot)	Community Optimized	Community Optimized	5.5 (includes Apache S...

Actions

Libraries / Spark UI / Logs | ▣   ↻   ⧉   🔒   ✕

Figure 1-13.   Cluster library

Within the Libraries tab, if the cluster already has a set of pre-installed libraries, they will be listed, or, in the case of a new cluster, no packages will be installed. We then click the Install New button (Figure 1-14).

Figure 1-14. *Installing a new library*

This will open a new window with multiple options to import or install a new library in Databricks (Figure 1-15). We select PyPI, and in the Package option, we mention the version of TensorFlow required to be installed, as shown in Figure 1-16.

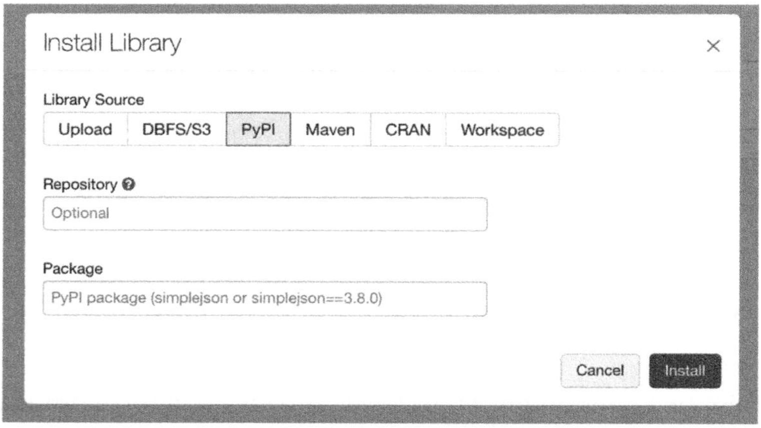

Figure 1-15. *PyPI source*

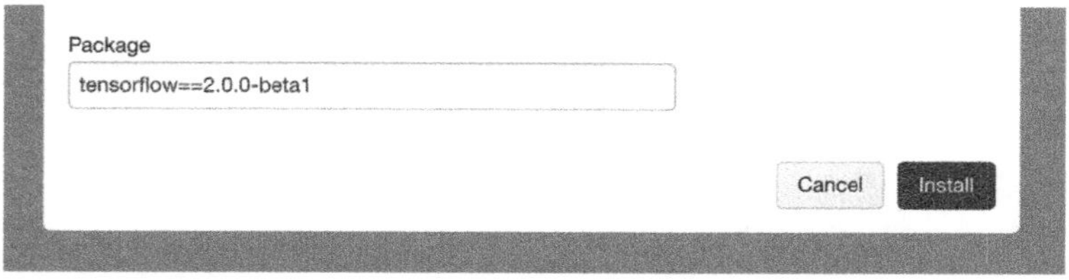

Figure 1-16. *TensorFlow package*

It will take some time, and we can then see TensorFlow successfully installed in Databricks, under Libraries. We can now open a new or existing notebook using the same cluster (Figures 1-17 and 1-18).

Figure 1-17. *Running cluster*

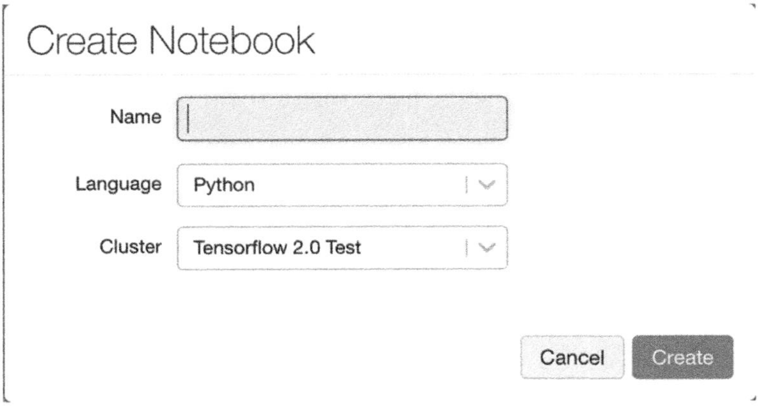

Figure 1-18. *New notebook*

The final step is simply to import TensorFlow in the notebook and validate the version. We can print the TensorFlow version, as shown in Figure 1-19.

Figure 1-19.   *TensorFlow notebook*

Conclusion

In this chapter, we explained the fundamental difference between a vector and a tensor. We also covered the major differences between previous and current versions of TensorFlow. Finally, we went over the process of installing TensorFlow locally as well as in a cloud environment (with Databricks).

CHAPTER 2

Supervised Learning with TensorFlow

In this chapter, we will be explaining the concept of supervised machine learning. Next, we take a deep dive into such supervised machine learning techniques as linear regression, logistic regression, and boosted trees. Finally, we will demonstrate all the aforementioned techniques, using TensorFlow 2.0.

What Is Supervised Machine Learning?

First, let us quickly review the concept of machine learning and then see what supervised machine learning is, with the help of an example.

As defined by Arthur Samuel in 1959, machine learning is the field of study that gives computers the ability to learn without being explicitly programmed. The aim of machine learning is to build programs whose performance improves automatically with some input parameters, such as data, performance criteria, etc. The programs become more data-driven, in terms of making decisions or predictions. We may not be aware of it, but machine learning has taken over our daily lives, from recommending products on online portals to self-driving cars that can take us from point A to point B without our driving them or employing a driver.

© Pramod Singh, Avinash Manure 2020
P. Singh and A. Manure, *Learn TensorFlow 2.0*,
https://doi.org/10.1007/978-1-4842-5558-2_2

Machine learning is a part of artificial intelligence (AI) and mainly comprises three types:

1. Supervised machine learning

2. Unsupervised machine learning

3. Reinforcement learning

Let us explore supervised machine learning via an example and then implement different techniques using TensorFlow 2.0. Note that unsupervised machine learning and reinforcement learning are beyond the scope of this book.

Imagine a three-year-old seeing a kitten for the first time. How would the child react? The child doesn't know what he/she is seeing. He or she might initially experience a feeling of curiosity, fear, or joy. It is only after his or her parents pet the kitten that the child realizes the animal might not harm him/her. Later, the child might be comfortable enough to hold the kitten and play with it. Now, the next time the child sees a kitten, he/she may instantly recognize it and start playing with it, without the initial fear or curiosity it felt toward the kitten previously. The child has *learned* that the kitten is not harmful, and, instead, he/she can play with it. This is how supervised learning works in real life.

In the machine world, supervised learning is done by providing a machine inputs and labels and asking it to learn from them. For example, using the preceding example, we can provide to the machine pictures of kittens, with the corresponding label (kitten), and ask it to learn the intrinsic features of a kitten, so that it can generalize well. Later, if we provide an image of another kitten without a label, the machine will be able to predict that the image is that of a kitten.

Supervised learning usually comprises two phases: training and testing/prediction. In the training phase, a set of the total data, called a training set, is provided to the machine learning algorithm, made up of input data (features) as well as output data (labels). The aim of the training phase is to make sure the algorithm learns as much as possible from the input data and forms a mapping between input and output, such that it can be used to make predictions. In the test/prediction phase, the remaining set of data, called a test set, is provided to the algorithm and comprises only the input data (features) and not the labels. The aim of the test/prediction phase is to check how well the model is able to learn and generalize. If the accuracy of the training and test sets differs too much, we can infer that the model might have mapped the input and output of training data too closely, and, therefore, it was not able to generalize the unseen data (test set) well. This is generally known as overfitting.

A typical supervised machine learning architecture is shown in Figure 2-1.

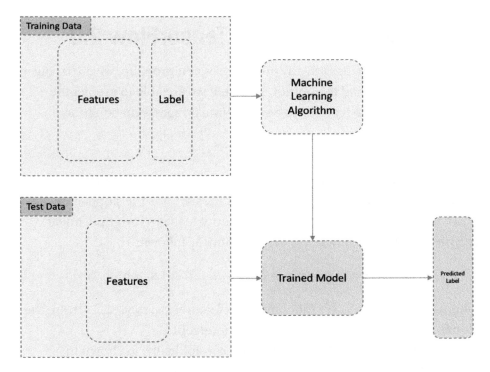

Figure 2-1. *Supervised machine learning architecture*

Within supervised learning, if we are to predict numeric values, this is called regression, whereas if we are to predict classes or categorical variables, we call that classification. For example, if the aim is to predict the sales (in dollars) a company is going to earn (numeric value), this comes under regression. If the aim is to determine whether a customer will buy a product from an online store or to check if an employee is going to churn or not (categorical yes or no), this is a classification problem.

Classification can be further divided as binary and multi-class. Binary classification deals with classifying two outcomes, i.e., either yes or no. Multi-class classification yields multiple outcomes. For example, a customer is categorized as a hot prospect, warm prospect, or cold prospect, etc.

Linear Regression with TensorFlow 2.0

In linear regression, as with any other regression problem, we are trying to map the inputs and the output, such that we are able to predict the numeric output. We try to form a simple linear regression equation:

$$y = mx + b$$

In this equation, y is the numeric output that we are interested in, and x is the input variable, i.e., part of the features set. m is the slope of the line, and b is the intercept. For multi-variate input features (multiple linear regression), we can generalize the equation, as follows:

$$y = m_1x_1 + m_2x_2 + m_3x_3 + \ldots\ldots + m_nx_n + b$$

where x_1, x_2, x_3, ..., x_n are different input features, m_1, m_2, m_3, ... m_n are the slopes for different features, and b is the intercept

This equation can also be represented graphically, as shown in Figure 2-2 (in 2D).

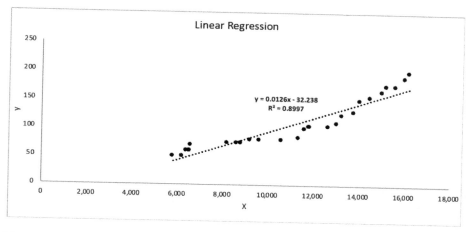

Figure 2-2. *Linear regression graph*

Here, we can clearly see that there is a linear relation between label y and feature inputs X.

Implementation of a Linear Regression Model, Using TensorFlow and Keras

We will implement the linear regression method in TensorFlow 2.0, using the Boston housing data set and the LinearRegressor estimator available within the TensorFlow package.

1. Import the required modules.

```
[In]: from __future__ import absolute_import, division, print_
function, unicode_literals
```

```
[In]: import numpy as np
[In]: import pandas as pd
[In]: import seaborn as sb
[In]: import tensorflow as tf
[In]: from tensorflow import keras as ks
```

```
[In]: from tensorflow.estimator import LinearRegressor
[In]: from sklearn import datasets
[In]: from sklearn.model_selection import train_test_split
[In]: from sklearn.metrics import mean_squared_error, r2_score
[In]: print(tf.__version__)
[Out]: 2.0.0-rc1
```

2.   Load and configure the Boston housing data set.

```
[In]: boston_load = datasets.load_boston()
[In]: feature_columns = boston_load.feature_names
[In]: target_column = boston_load.target
[In]: boston_data = pd.DataFrame(boston_load.data,
        columns=feature_columns).astype(np.float32)
[In]: boston_data['MEDV'] = target_column.astype(np.float32)
[In]: boston_data.head()
```

[Out]:

	CRIM	ZN	INDUS	CHAS	NOX	RM	AGE	DIS	RAD	TAX	PTRATIO	B	LSTAT	MEDV
0	0.00632	18.0	2.31	0.0	0.538	6.575	65.199997	4.0900	1.0	296.0	15.300000	396.899994	4.98	24.000000
1	0.02731	0.0	7.07	0.0	0.469	6.421	78.900002	4.9671	2.0	242.0	17.799999	396.899994	9.14	21.600000
2	0.02729	0.0	7.07	0.0	0.469	7.185	61.099998	4.9671	2.0	242.0	17.799999	392.829987	4.03	34.700001
3	0.03237	0.0	2.18	0.0	0.458	6.998	45.799999	6.0622	3.0	222.0	18.700001	394.630005	2.94	33.400002
4	0.06905	0.0	2.18	0.0	0.458	7.147	54.200001	6.0622	3.0	222.0	18.700001	396.899994	5.33	36.200001

3.   Check the relation between the variables, using
     pairplot and a correlation graph.

```
[In]: sb.pairplot(boston_data, diag_kind="kde")
[Out]:
```

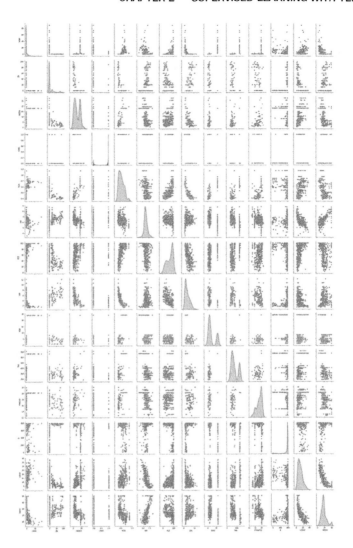

```
[In]: correlation_data = boston_data.corr()
[In]: correlation_data.style.background_
      gradient(cmap='coolwarm', axis=None)
[Out]:
```

	CRIM	ZN	INDUS	CHAS	NOX	RM	AGE	DIS	RAD	TAX	PTRATIO	B	LSTAT	MEDV
CRIM	1	-0.200469	0.406583	-0.0558916	0.420972	-0.219247	0.352734	-0.37967	0.625505	0.582764	0.289946	-0.385064	0.455621	-0.388305
ZN	-0.200469	1	-0.533828	-0.0426967	-0.516604	0.311991	-0.569537	0.664408	-0.311948	-0.314563	-0.391679	0.17552	-0.412995	0.360445
INDUS	0.406583	-0.533828	1	0.062938	0.763651	-0.391676	0.644779	-0.708027	0.595129	0.72076	0.383248	-0.356977	0.6038	-0.483725
CHAS	-0.0558916	-0.0426967	0.062938	1	0.0912028	0.0912512	0.0865178	-0.0991758	-0.00736824	-0.0355865	-0.121515	0.0487885	-0.0539293	0.17526
NOX	0.420972	-0.516604	0.763651	0.0912028	1	-0.302188	0.73147	-0.76923	0.611441	0.668023	0.188933	-0.380051	0.590879	-0.427321
RM	-0.219247	0.311991	-0.391676	0.0912512	-0.302188	1	-0.240265	0.205246	-0.209847	-0.292048	-0.355502	0.128069	-0.613808	0.69536
AGE	0.352734	-0.569537	0.644779	0.0865178	0.73147	-0.240265	1	-0.747881	0.456022	0.506456	0.261515	-0.273534	0.602339	-0.376955
DIS	-0.37967	0.664408	-0.708027	-0.0991758	-0.76923	0.205246	-0.747881	1	-0.494588	-0.534432	-0.232471	0.291512	-0.496996	0.249929
RAD	0.625505	-0.311948	0.595129	-0.00736824	0.611441	-0.209847	0.456022	-0.494588	1	0.910228	0.464741	-0.444413	0.488676	-0.381626
TAX	0.582764	-0.314563	0.72076	-0.0355865	0.668023	-0.292048	0.506456	-0.534432	0.910228	1	0.460853	-0.441808	0.543993	-0.468536
PTRATIO	0.289946	-0.391679	0.383248	-0.121515	0.188933	-0.355502	0.261515	-0.232471	0.464741	0.460853	1	-0.177383	0.374044	-0.507787
B	-0.385064	0.17552	-0.356977	0.0487885	-0.380051	0.128069	-0.273534	0.291512	-0.444413	-0.441808	-0.177383	1	-0.366087	0.333461
LSTAT	0.455621	-0.412995	0.6038	-0.0539293	0.590879	-0.613808	0.602339	-0.496996	0.488676	0.543993	0.374044	-0.366087	1	-0.737663
MEDV	-0.388305	0.360445	-0.483725	0.17526	-0.427321	0.69536	-0.376955	0.249929	-0.381626	-0.468536	-0.507787	0.333461	-0.737663	1

4. Descriptive statistics—central tendency and dispersion

```
[In]:  stats = boston_data.describe()
[In]: boston_stats = stats.transpose()
[In]: boston_stats
[Out]:
```

	count	mean	std	min	25%	50%	75%	max
CRIM	506.0	3.613523	8.601545	0.00632	0.082045	0.256510	3.677083	88.976196
ZN	506.0	11.363636	23.322390	0.00000	0.000000	0.000000	12.500000	100.000000
INDUS	506.0	11.136797	6.860355	0.46000	5.190000	9.690000	18.100000	27.740000
CHAS	506.0	0.069170	0.253993	0.00000	0.000000	0.000000	0.000000	1.000000
NOX	506.0	0.554696	0.115878	0.38500	0.449000	0.538000	0.624000	0.871000
RM	506.0	6.284636	0.702617	3.56100	5.885500	6.208500	6.623500	8.780000
AGE	506.0	68.574921	28.148869	2.90000	45.025000	77.500000	94.074999	100.000000
DIS	506.0	3.795043	2.105711	1.12960	2.100175	3.207450	5.188425	12.126500
RAD	506.0	9.549407	8.707269	1.00000	4.000000	5.000000	24.000000	24.000000
TAX	506.0	408.237152	168.537170	187.00000	279.000000	330.000000	666.000000	711.000000
PTRATIO	506.0	18.455584	2.164946	12.60000	17.400000	19.050000	20.200001	22.000000
B	506.0	356.674561	91.294838	0.32000	375.377487	391.440002	396.225006	396.899994
LSTAT	506.0	12.653064	7.141063	1.73000	6.950000	11.360000	16.954999	37.970001
MEDV	506.0	22.532806	9.197104	5.00000	17.025000	21.200001	25.000000	50.000000

5. Select the required columns.

```
[In]:  X_data = boston_data[[i for i in boston_data.columns if
       i not in ['MEDV']]]
[In]:  Y_data = boston_data[['MEDV']]
```

6. Train the test split.

```
[In]:  training_features , test_features ,training_labels, test_
       labels = train_test_split(X_data , Y_data , test_size=0.2)
[In]:  print('No. of rows in Training Features: ', training_
       features.shape[0])
[In]:  print('No. of rows in Test Features: ', test_features.
       shape[0])
[In]:  print('No. of columns in Training Features: ', training_
       features.shape[1])
[In]:  print('No. of columns in Test Features: ', test_
       features.shape[1])
[In]:  print('No. of rows in Training Label: ', training_
       labels.shape[0])
[In]:  print('No. of rows in Test Label: ', test_labels.shape[0])
[In]:  print('No. of columns in Training Label: ', training_
       labels.shape[1])
[In]:  print('No. of columns in Test Label: ', test_labels.shape[1])
[Out]:
```

```
No. of rows in Training Features:  404
No. of rows in Test Features:  102
No. of columns in Training Features:  13
No. of columns in Test Features:  13
No. of rows in Training Label:  404
No. of rows in Test Label:  102
No. of columns in Training Label:  1
No. of columns in Test Label:  1
```

7.   Normalize the data.

```
[In]: def norm(x):
         stats = x.describe()
         stats = stats.transpose()
         return (x - stats['mean']) / stats['std']

[In]: normed_train_features = norm(training_features)
[In]: normed_test_features = norm(test_features)
```

8.   Build the input pipeline for the TensorFlow model.

```
[In]: def feed_input(features_dataframe, target_dataframe,
       num_of_epochs=10, shuffle=True, batch_size=32):
            def input_feed_function():
                dataset = tf.data.Dataset.from_tensor_slices
                ((dict(features_dataframe), target_dataframe))
                if shuffle:
                     dataset = dataset.shuffle(2000)
                dataset = dataset.batch(batch_size).repeat
                (num_of_epochs)
                return dataset
            return input_feed_function
[In]: train_feed_input = feed_input(normed_train_features,
       training_labels)
[In]: train_feed_input_testing = feed_input(normed_train_features,
[In]: training_labels, num_of_epochs=1, shuffle=False)
[In]: test_feed_input = feed_input(normed_test_features,
       test_labels, num_of_epochs=1, shuffle=False)
```

9.   Model training

```
[In]: feature_columns_numeric = [tf.feature_column.numeric_
      column(m) for m in training_features.columns]
[In]: linear_model = LinearRegressor(feature_columns=feature_
      columns_numeric, optimizer='RMSProp')
[In]: linear_model.train(train_feed_input)
[Out]:
```

```
INFO:tensorflow:Graph was finalized.
INFO:tensorflow:Running local_init_op.
INFO:tensorflow:Done running local_init_op.
INFO:tensorflow:Saving checkpoints for 0 into /tmp/tmp8tuc4emt/model.ckpt.
INFO:tensorflow:loss = 491.5925, step = 0
INFO:tensorflow:global_step/sec: 174.222
INFO:tensorflow:loss = 27.792591, step = 100 (0.576 sec)
INFO:tensorflow:Saving checkpoints for 130 into /tmp/tmp8tuc4emt/model.ckpt.
INFO:tensorflow:Loss for final step: 30.763996.
<tensorflow_estimator.python.estimator.canned.linear.LinearRegressorV2 at 0x7fa81c556be0>
```

10.   Predictions

```
[In]: train_predictions = linear_model.predict(train_feed_
      input_testing)
[In]: test_predictions = linear_model.predict(test_feed_input)
[In]: train_predictions_series = pd.Series([p['predictions'][0]
      for p in train_predictions])
[In]: test_predictions_series = pd.Series([p['predictions'][0]
      for p in test_predictions])
[Out]:
```

```
INFO:tensorflow:Calling model_fn.
INFO:tensorflow:Done calling model_fn.
INFO:tensorflow:Graph was finalized.
INFO:tensorflow:Restoring parameters from /tmp/tmp8tuc4emt/model.ckpt-130
INFO:tensorflow:Running local_init_op.
INFO:tensorflow:Done running local_init_op.
INFO:tensorflow:Calling model_fn.
INFO:tensorflow:Done calling model_fn.
INFO:tensorflow:Graph was finalized.
INFO:tensorflow:Restoring parameters from /tmp/tmp8tuc4emt/model.ckpt-130
INFO:tensorflow:Running local_init_op.
INFO:tensorflow:Done running local_init_op.
```

```
[In]: train_predictions_df = pd.DataFrame(train_predictions_
      series, columns=['predictions'])
[In]: test_predictions_df = pd.DataFrame(test_predictions_
      series, columns=['predictions'])
[In]: training_labels.reset_index(drop=True, inplace=True)
[In]: train_predictions_df.reset_index(drop=True, inplace=True)
[In]: test_labels.reset_index(drop=True, inplace=True)
[In]: test_predictions_df.reset_index(drop=True, inplace=True)
[In]: train_labels_with_predictions_df = pd.concat([training_
      labels, train_predictions_df], axis=1)
[In]: test_labels_with_predictions_df = pd.concat([test_labels,
      test_predictions_df], axis=1)
```

11. Validation

```
[In]: def calculate_errors_and_r2(y_true, y_pred):
          mean_squared_err = (mean_squared_error(y_true, y_pred))
          root_mean_squared_err = np.sqrt(mean_squared_err)
          r2 = round(r2_score(y_true, y_pred)*100,0)
          return mean_squared_err, root_mean_squared_err, r2
[In]: train_mean_squared_error, train_root_mean_squared_error,
      train_r2_score_percentage = calculate_errors_and_
      r2(training_labels, train_predictions_series)
[In]: test_mean_squared_error, test_root_mean_squared_error,
      test_r2_score_percentage = calculate_errors_and_r2(test_
      labels, test_predictions_series)
[In]: print('Training Data Mean Squared Error = ', train_mean_
      squared_error)
[In]: print('Training Data Root Mean Squared Error = ', train_
      root_mean_squared_error)
[In]: print('Training Data R2 = ', train_r2_score_percentage)
```

```
[In]: print('Test Data Mean Squared Error = ', test_mean_
      squared_error)
[In]: print('Test Data Root Mean Squared Error = ', test_root_
      mean_squared_error)
[In]: print('Test Data R2 = ', test_r2_score_percentage)
[Out]:
```

```
Training Data Mean Squared Error =   22.418754587521754
Training Data Root Mean Squared Error =   4.734844726865048
Training Data R2 =   72.0
Test Data Mean Squared Error =   30.361685998071252
Test Data Root Mean Squared Error =   5.510143918090638
Test Data R2 =   69.0
```

The code for the linear regression implementation using TensorFlow 2.0 can be found here: http://bit.ly/LinRegTF2. You can save a copy of the code, run it in the Google Colab environment, and try experimenting with different parameters, to see the results.

Logistic Regression with TensorFlow 2.0

Logistic regression is one of the most popular classification methods. Although the name contains *regression*, and the underlying method is the same as that for linear regression, it is not a regression method. That is, it is not used for prediction of continuous (numeric) values. The purpose of the logistic regression method is to predict the outcome, which is categorical.

As mentioned, logistic regression's underlying method is the same as that for linear regression. Suppose we take the multi-class linear equation, as shown following:

$$y = m_1x_1 + m_2x_2 + m_3x_3 + \ldots\ldots\ldots + m_nx_n + b$$

where x_1, x_2, x_3, ..., x_n are different input features, m_1, m_2, m_3, ... m_n are the slopes for different features, and **b** is the intercept.

We will apply a logistic function to the linear equation, as follows:

$$p(y=1) = 1/\left(1 + e^{-(m_1x_1 + m_2x_2 + m_3x_3 + \ldots + m_nx_n + b)}\right)$$

where $p(y=1)$ is the probability value of $y=1$.

If we plot this function, it will look like an S, hence it is called a sigmoid function (Figure 2-3).

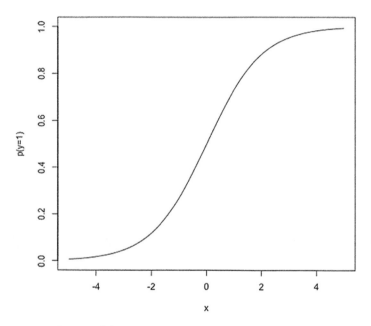

Figure 2-3. *A sigmoid function representation*

We will implement the logistic regression method in TensorFlow 2.0, using the iris data set and the LinearClassifier estimator available within the TensorFlow package.

1. Import the required modules.

```
[In]: from __future__ import absolute_import, division, print_
      function, unicode_literals
[In]: import pandas as pd
[In]: import seaborn as sb
[In]: import tensorflow as tf
[In]: from tensorflow import keras
[In]: from tensorflow.estimator import LinearClassifier
[In]: from sklearn.model_selection import train_test_split
[In]: from sklearn.metrics import accuracy_score, precision_
      score, recall_score
[In]: print(tf.__version__)
[Out]: 2.0.0-rc1
```

2. Load and configure the iris data set.

```
[In]: col_names = ['SepalLength', 'SepalWidth', 'PetalLength',
      'PetalWidth', 'Species']
[In]: target_dimensions = ['Setosa', 'Versicolor', 'Virginica']
[In]: training_data_path = tf.keras.utils.get_file("iris_
      training.csv", "https://storage.googleapis.com/download.
      tensorflow.org/data/iris_training.csv")
[In]: test_data_path = tf.keras.utils.get_file("iris_test.csv",
      "https://storage.googleapis.com/download.tensorflow.org/
      data/iris_test.csv")
[In]: training = pd.read_csv(training_data_path, names=col_
      names, header=0)
[In]: training = training[training['Species'] >= 1]
[In]: training['Species'] = training['Species'].replace([1,2], [0,1])
[In]: test = pd.read_csv(test_data_path, names=col_names,
      header=0)
```

```
[In]: test = test[test['Species'] >= 1]
[In]: test['Species'] = test['Species'].replace([1,2], [0,1])
[In]: training.reset_index(drop=True, inplace=True)
[In]: test.reset_index(drop=True, inplace=True)
[In]: iris_dataset = pd.concat([training, test], axis=0)
[In]: iris_dataset.describe()
[Out]:
```

	SepalLength	SepalWidth	PetalLength	PetalWidth	Species
count	100.000000	100.000000	100.000000	100.000000	100.000000
mean	6.262000	2.872000	4.906000	1.676000	0.500000
std	0.662834	0.332751	0.825578	0.424769	0.502519
min	4.900000	2.000000	3.000000	1.000000	0.000000
25%	5.800000	2.700000	4.375000	1.300000	0.000000
50%	6.300000	2.900000	4.900000	1.600000	0.500000
75%	6.700000	3.025000	5.525000	2.000000	1.000000
max	7.900000	3.800000	6.900000	2.500000	1.000000

3. Check the relation between the variables, using
    pairplot and a correlation graph.

```
[In]: sb.pairplot(iris_dataset, diag_kind="kde")
[Out]:
```

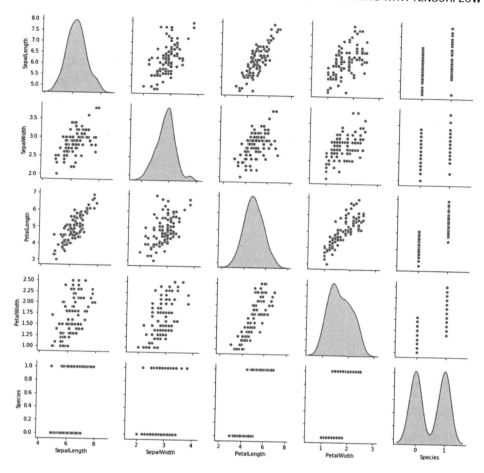

```
[In]:  correlation_data = iris_dataset.corr()
[In]:  correlation_data.style.background_gradient(cmap='coolwarm',
       axis=None)
```

[Out]:

	SepalLength	SepalWidth	PetalLength	PetalWidth	Species
SepalLength	1	0.553855	0.828479	0.593709	0.494305
SepalWidth	0.553855	1	0.519802	0.566203	0.30808
PetalLength	0.828479	0.519802	1	0.823348	0.786424
PetalWidth	0.593709	0.566203	0.823348	1	0.828129
Species	0.494305	0.30808	0.786424	0.828129	1

    4.   Descriptive statistics—central tendency and dispersion

```
[In]:  stats = iris_dataset.describe()
[In]: iris_stats = stats.transpose()
[In]: iris_stats
[Out]:
```

	count	mean	std	min	25%	50%	75%	max
SepalLength	100.0	6.262	0.662834	4.9	5.800	6.3	6.700	7.9
SepalWidth	100.0	2.872	0.332751	2.0	2.700	2.9	3.025	3.8
PetalLength	100.0	4.906	0.825578	3.0	4.375	4.9	5.525	6.9
PetalWidth	100.0	1.676	0.424769	1.0	1.300	1.6	2.000	2.5
Species	100.0	0.500	0.502519	0.0	0.000	0.5	1.000	1.0

    5.   Select the required columns.

```
[In]: X_data = iris_dataset[[i for i in iris_dataset.columns if
      i not in ['Species']]]
[In]:  Y_data = iris_dataset[['Species']]
```

6. Train the test split.

```
[In]:   training_features , test_features ,training_labels, test_
        labels = train_test_split(X_data , Y_data , test_size=0.2)
[In]: print('No. of rows in Training Features: ', training_
      features.shape[0])
[In]: print('No. of rows in Test Features: ', test_features.
      shape[0])
[In]: print('No. of columns in Training Features: ', training_
      features.shape[1])
[In]: print('No. of columns in Test Features: ', test_features.
      shape[1])
[In]: print('No. of rows in Training Label: ', training_labels.
      shape[0])
[In]: print('No. of rows in Test Label: ', test_labels.shape[0])
[In]: print('No. of columns in Training Label: ', training_
      labels.shape[1])
[In]: print('No. of columns in Test Label: ', test_labels.
      shape[1])
[Out]:
```

```
No. of rows in Training Features:  80
No. of rows in Test Features:  20
No. of columns in Training Features:  4
No. of columns in Test Features:  4
No. of rows in Training Label:  80
No. of rows in Test Label:  20
No. of columns in Training Label:  1
No. of columns in Test Label:  1
```

7. Normalize the data.

```
[In]: def norm(x):
          stats = x.describe()
          stats = stats.transpose()
          return (x - stats['mean']) / stats['std']
[In]: normed_train_features = norm(training_features)
[In]: normed_test_features = norm(test_features)
```

8. Build the input pipeline for the TensorFlow model.

```
[In]: def feed_input(features_dataframe, target_dataframe,
      num_of_epochs=10, shuffle=True, batch_size=32):
          def input_feed_function():
              dataset = tf.data.Dataset.from_tensor_slices
              ((dict(features_dataframe), target_dataframe))
              if shuffle:
                  dataset = dataset.shuffle(2000)
              dataset = dataset.batch(batch_size).
              repeat(num_of_epochs)
              return dataset
          return input_feed_function
[In]: train_feed_input = feed_input(normed_train_features,
      training_labels)
[In]: train_feed_input_testing = feed_input(normed_train_features,
      training_labels, num_of_epochs=1, shuffle=False)
[In]: test_feed_input = feed_input(normed_test_features,
      test_labels, num_of_epochs=1, shuffle=False)
```

9. Model training

```
[In]: feature_columns_numeric = [tf.feature_column.numeric_
      column(m) for m in training_features.columns]
[In]:logistic_model = LinearClassifier (feature_
      columns=feature_columns_numeric)
[In]: logistic_model.train(train_feed_input)
[Out]:
```

```
INFO:tensorflow:Done calling model_fn.
INFO:tensorflow:Create CheckpointSaverHook.
INFO:tensorflow:Graph was finalized.
INFO:tensorflow:Running local_init_op.
INFO:tensorflow:Done running local_init_op.
INFO:tensorflow:Saving checkpoints for 0 into /tmp/tmpzujy116g/model.ckpt.
INFO:tensorflow:loss = 0.6931472, step = 0
INFO:tensorflow:Saving checkpoints for 30 into /tmp/tmpzujy116g/model.ckpt.
INFO:tensorflow:Loss for final step: 0.18215306.
<tensorflow_estimator.python.estimator.canned.linear.LinearClassifierV2 at 0x7f0401d66e80>
```

10. Predictions

```
[In]: train_predictions = logistic_model.predict(train_feed_
      input_testing)
[In]: test_predictions = logistic_model.predict(test_feed_input)
[In]: train_predictions_series = pd.Series([p['classes'][0].
      decode("utf-8")   for p in train_predictions])
[In]: test_predictions_series = pd.Series([p['classes'][0].
      decode("utf-8")   for p in test_predictions])
[Out]:
```

```
INFO:tensorflow:Done calling model_fn.
INFO:tensorflow:Graph was finalized.
INFO:tensorflow:Restoring parameters from /tmp/tmpzujy116g/model.ckpt-30
INFO:tensorflow:Running local_init_op.
INFO:tensorflow:Done running local_init_op.
```

```
[In]: train_predictions_df = pd.DataFrame(train_predictions_
      series, columns=['predictions'])
```

```
[In]: test_predictions_df = pd.DataFrame(test_predictions_
      series, columns=['predictions'])
[In]: training_labels.reset_index(drop=True, inplace=True)
[In]: train_predictions_df.reset_index(drop=True, inplace=True)
[In]: test_labels.reset_index(drop=True, inplace=True)
[In]: test_predictions_df.reset_index(drop=True, inplace=True)
[In]: train_labels_with_predictions_df = pd.concat([training_
      labels, train_predictions_df], axis=1)
[In]: test_labels_with_predictions_df = pd.concat([test_labels,
      test_predictions_df], axis=1)
```

11. Validation

```
[In]: def calculate_binary_class_scores(y_true, y_pred):
          accuracy = accuracy_score(y_true, y_pred.astype('int64'))
          precision = precision_score(y_true, y_pred.astype('int64'))
          recall = recall_score(y_true, y_pred.astype('int64'))
          return accuracy, precision, recall
[In]: train_accuracy_score, train_precision_score, train_
      recall_score = calculate_binary_class_scores(training_
      labels, train_predictions_series)
[In]: test_accuracy_score, test_precision_score, test_recall_
      score = calculate_binary_class_scores(test_labels, test_
      predictions_series)
[In]: print('Training Data Accuracy (%) = ', round(train_
      accuracy_score*100,2))
[In]: print('Training Data Precision (%) = ', round(train_
      precision_score*100,2))
[In]: print('Training Data Recall (%) = ', round(train_recall_
      score*100,2))
[In]: print('-'*50)
```

```
[In]: print('Test Data Accuracy (%) = ', round(test_accuracy_
      score*100,2))
[In]: print('Test Data Precision (%) = ', round(test_precision_
      score*100,2))
[In]: print('Test Data Recall (%) = ', round(test_recall_
      score*100,2))
[Out]:

    Training Data Accuracy (%) =  96.25
    Training Data Precision (%) =  97.5
    Training Data Recall (%) =  95.12
    -----------------------------------------------------
    Test Data Accuracy (%) =  90.0
    Test Data Precision (%) =  81.82
    Test Data Recall (%) =  100.0
```

The code for the logistic regression implementation using TensorFlow 2.0 can be found at http://bit.ly/LogRegTF2. You can save a copy of the code and run it in the Google Colab environment. Try experimenting with different parameters and note the results.

Boosted Trees with TensorFlow 2.0

Before we implement the boosted trees method in TensorFlow 2.0, we want to quickly highlight related key terms.

Ensemble Technique

An ensemble is a collection of predictors. For example, instead of using a single model (say, logistic regression) for a classification problem, we can use multiple models (say, logistic regression + decision trees, etc.) to perform predictions. The outputs from the predictors are combined by different averaging methods, such as weighted averages, normal averages, or votes, and a final prediction value is derived. Ensemble methods have been proved to be more effective than individual methods and, therefore, are heavily used to build machine learning models. Ensemble methods can be implemented by either bagging or boosting.

Bagging

Bagging is a technique wherein we build independent models/predictors, using a random subsample/bootstrap of data for each of the models/predictors. Then an average (weighted, normal, or by voting) of the scores from the different predictors is taken to get the final score/prediction. The most famous bagging method is random forest.

A typical bagging technique is depicted in Figure 2-4.

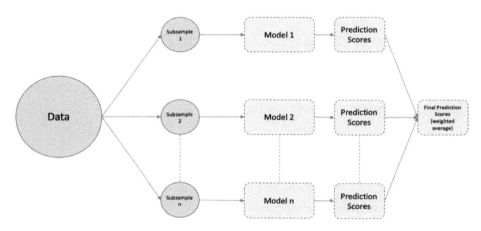

Figure 2-4. *Bagging technique*

Boosting

Boosting is a different ensemble technique, wherein the predictors are not independently trained but done so in a sequential manner. For example, we build a logistic regression model on a subsample/bootstrap of the original training data set. Then we take the output of this model and feed it to a decision tree, to get the prediction, and so on. The aim of this sequential training is for the subsequent models to learn from the mistakes of the previous model. Gradient boosting is an example of a boosting method.

A typical boosting technique is depicted in Figure 2-5.

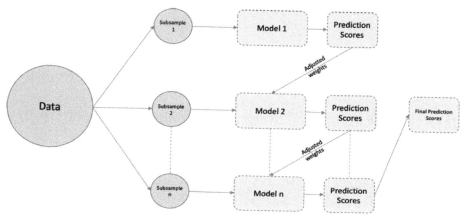

Figure 2-5. *Boosting technique*

Gradient Boosting

The main difference between gradient boosting compared to other boosting methods is that instead of incrementing the weights of misclassified outcomes from one previous learner to the next, we optimize the loss function of the previous learner.

We will be building a boosted trees classifier, using the gradient boosting method under the hood. We will take the iris data set for classification. As we have already used the same data set for implementing logistic regression in the previous section, we will keep the preprocessing the same (i.e., until the "Build the input pipeline for TensorFlow model" step from the previous example). We will continue directly with the model training step, as follows:

1. Model training

```
[In]: from tensorflow.estimator import BoostedTreesClassifier
[In]: btree_model = BoostedTreesClassifier(feature_
      columns=feature_columns_numeric, n_batches_per_layer=1)
[In]: btree_model.train(train_feed_input)
```

2. Predictions

```
[In]: train_predictions = btree_model.predict(train_feed_input_
      testing)
[In]: test_predictions = btree_model.predict(test_feed_input)
[In]: train_predictions_series = pd.Series([p['classes'][0].
      decode("utf-8")   for p in train_predictions])
[In]: test_predictions_series = pd.Series([p['classes'][0].
      decode("utf-8")   for p in test_predictions])
[Out]:
```

```
INFO:tensorflow:Calling model_fn.
INFO:tensorflow:Done calling model_fn.
INFO:tensorflow:Graph was finalized.
INFO:tensorflow:Restoring parameters from /tmp/tmp2r0_p6eo/model.ckpt-19
INFO:tensorflow:Running local_init_op.
INFO:tensorflow:Done running local_init_op.
INFO:tensorflow:Calling model_fn.
INFO:tensorflow:Done calling model_fn.
INFO:tensorflow:Graph was finalized.
INFO:tensorflow:Restoring parameters from /tmp/tmp2r0_p6eo/model.ckpt-19
INFO:tensorflow:Running local_init_op.
INFO:tensorflow:Done running local_init_op.
```

```
[In]: train_predictions_df = pd.DataFrame(train_predictions_
      series, columns=['predictions'])
[In]: test_predictions_df = pd.DataFrame(test_predictions_
      series, columns=['predictions'])
[In]: training_labels.reset_index(drop=True, inplace=True)
[In]: train_predictions_df.reset_index(drop=True, inplace=True)
```

```
[In]: test_labels.reset_index(drop=True, inplace=True)
[In]: test_predictions_df.reset_index(drop=True, inplace=True)
[In]: train_labels_with_predictions_df = pd.concat([train_
      labels, train_predictions_df], axis=1)
[In]: test_labels_with_predictions_df = pd.concat([test_labels,
      test_predictions_df], axis=1)
```

3. Validation

```
[In]: def calculate_binary_class_scores(y_true, y_pred):
      accuracy = accuracy_score(y_true, y_pred.astype('int64'))
      precision = precision_score(y_true, y_pred.astype('int64'))
      recall = recall_score(y_true, y_pred.astype('int64'))
      return accuracy, precision, recall
[In]: train_accuracy_score, train_precision_score, train_
      recall_score = calculate_binary_class_scores(training_
      labels, train_predictions_series)
[In]: test_accuracy_score, test_precision_score, test_recall_
      score = calculate_binary_class_scores(test_labels, test_
      predictions_series)
[In]: print('Training Data Accuracy (%) = ', round(train_
      accuracy_score*100,2))
[In]: print('Training Data Precision (%) = ', round(train_
      precision_score*100,2))
[In]: print('Training Data Recall (%) = ', round(train_recall_
      score*100,2))
[In]: print('-'*50)
[In]: print('Test Data Accuracy (%) = ', round(test_accuracy_
      score*100,2))
[In]: print('Test Data Precision (%) = ', round(test_precision_
      score*100,2))
```

```
[In]: print('Test Data Recall (%) = ', round(test_recall_
      score*100,2))
[Out]:
```

```
      Training Data Accuracy (%)  =   98.57
      Training Data Precision (%) =   97.44
      Training Data Recall (%)  =   100.0
      --------------------------------------------------
      Test Data Accuracy (%)  =   93.33
      Test Data Precision (%) =   85.71
      Test Data Recall (%)  =   100.0
```

The code for the boosted trees implementation using TensorFlow 2.0 can be found at `http://bit.ly/GBTF2`. You can save a copy of the code and run it in the Google Colab environment. Try experimenting with different parameters and note the results.

Conclusion

You just saw how easy it has become to implement supervised machine learning algorithms in TensorFlow 2.0. You can build the models just as you would using the `scikit-learn` package. The Keras implementation within TensorFlow also makes it easy to build neural network models, which will be discussed in Chapter 3.

CHAPTER 3

Neural Networks and Deep Learning with TensorFlow

This chapter focuses on neural networks and how we can build them to perform machine learning, by closely mimicking the human brain. We will start by determining what neural networks are and how similarly they are structured to the neural network in humans. Then, we will deep dive into the architecture of neural networks, exploring the different layers within. We will explain how a simple neural network is built and delve into the concepts of forward and backward propagation. Later, we will build a simple neural network, using TensorFlow and Keras. In the final sections of this chapter, we will discuss deep neural networks, how they differ from simple neural networks, and how to implement deep neural networks with TensorFlow and Keras, again with performance comparisons to simple neural networks.

What Are Neural Networks?

Neural networks are a type of machine learning algorithm that tries to mimic the human brain. Computers always have been better at performing complex computations, compared to humans. They can do the calculations

© Pramod Singh, Avinash Manure 2020
P. Singh and A. Manure, *Learn TensorFlow 2.0*,
https://doi.org/10.1007/978-1-4842-5558-2_3

in no time, whereas for humans, it takes a while to perform even the simplest of operations manually. Then why do we need machines to mimic the human brain? The reason is that humans have common sense and imagination. They can be inspired by something to which computers cannot. If the computational capability of computers is combined with the common sense and imagination of humans, which can function continually 365 days a year, what is created? Superhumans? The response to those questions defines the whole purpose of artificial intelligence (AI).

Neurons

The human body consists of neurons, which are the basic building blocks of the nervous system. A neuron consists of a cell body, or soma, a single axon, and dendrites (Figure 3-1). Neurons are connected to one another by the dendrites and axon terminals. A signal from one neuron is passed to the axon terminal and dendrites of another connected neuron, which receives it and passes it through the soma, axon, and terminal, and so on.

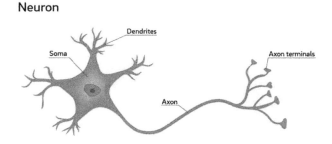

Figure 3-1. *Structure of a neuron (Source:* `https://bit.ly/2zOekEL`*)*

Neurons are interconnected in such a way that they have different functions, such as sensory neurons, which respond to such stimuli as sound, touch, or light; motor neurons, which control the muscle movements in the body; and interneurons, which are connected neurons within the same region of the brain or spinal cord.

Artificial Neural Networks (ANNs)

An artificial neural network tries to mimic the brain at its most basic level, i.e., that of the neuron. An artificial neuron has a similar structure to that of a human neuron and comprises the following sections (Figure 3-2):

> *Input layer*: This layer is similar to dendrites and takes input from other networks/neurons.
>
> *Summation layer*: This layer functions like the soma of neurons. It aggregates the input signal received.
>
> *Activation layer*: This layer is also similar to a soma, and it takes the aggregated information and fires a signal only if the aggregated input crosses a certain threshold value. Otherwise, it does not fire.
>
> *Output layer*: This layer is similar to axon terminals in that it might be connected to other neurons/networks or act as a final output layer (for predictions).

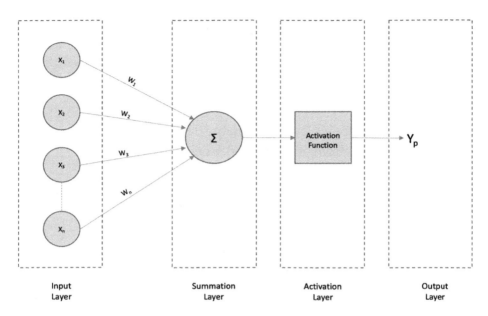

Figure 3-2. *Artificial neural network*

In the preceding figure, X_1, X_2, X_3,..........X_n are the inputs fed to the neural network. W_1, W_2, W_3,............W_n are the weights associated with the inputs, and Y is the final prediction.

Many activation functions can be used in the activation layer, to convert all the linear details produced at the input and make the summation layer nonlinear. This helps users acquire more details about the input data that would not be possible if this were a linear function. Therefore, the activation layer plays an important role in predictions. Some of the most familiar types of activation functions are sigmoid, ReLU, and softmax.

Simple Neural Network Architecture

As shown in Figure 3-3, a typical neural network architecture is made up of an

Input layer

Hidden layer

Output layer

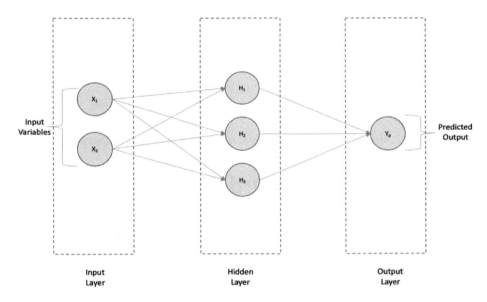

Figure 3-3. *Simple neural network architecture—regression*

Every input is connected to every neuron of the hidden layer and, in turn, connected to the output layer. If we are solving a regression problem, the architecture looks like the one shown in Figure 3-3, in which we have the output Y_p, which is continuous if predicted at the output layer. If we are solving a classification (binary, in this case), we will have the outputs Y_{class1} and Y_{class2}, which are the probability values for each of the binary classes 1 and 2 at the output layer, as shown in Figure 3-4.

57

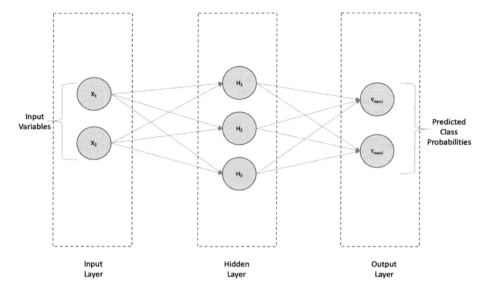

Figure 3-4. *Simple neural network architecture—classification*

Forward and Backward Propagation

In a fully connected neural network, when the inputs pass through the neurons (hidden layer to output layer), and the final value is calculated at the output layer, we say that the inputs have *forward propagated* (Figure 3-5). Consider, for example, a fully connected neural network with two inputs, X_1 and X_2, and one hidden layer with three neurons and an output layer with a single output Y_p (numeric value).

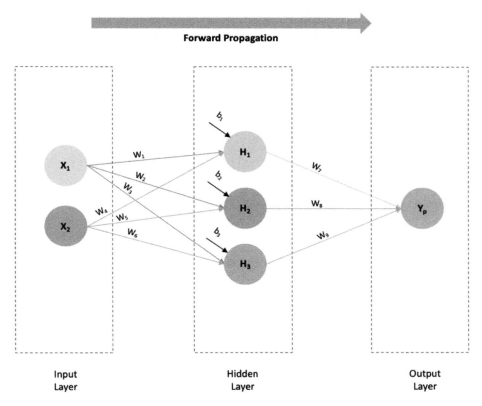

Figure 3-5. *Forward propagation*

The inputs will be fed to each of the hidden layer neurons, by multiplying each input value with a weight (W) and summing them with a bias value (b). So, the equations at the neurons' hidden layer will be as follows:

$$H_1 = W_1 * X_1 + W_4 * X_2 + b_1$$
$$H_2 = W_2 * X_1 + W_5 * X_2 + b_2$$
$$H_3 = W_3 * X_1 + W_6 * X_2 + b_3$$

The values H_1, H_2, and H_3 will be passed to the output layer, with weights W_7, W_8, and W_9, respectively. The output layer will produce the final predicted value of Y_p.

$$Y_p = W_7 * H_1 + W_8 * H_2 + W_9 * H_3$$

As the input data (X_1 and X_2) in this network flows in a forward direction to produce the final outcome, Y_p, it is said to be a feed forward network, or, because the data is propagating in a forward manner, a *forward propagation.*

Now, suppose the actual value of the output is known (denoted by Y). In this case, we can calculate the difference between the actual value and the predicted value, i.e., $L = (Y - Y_p)^2$, where L is the loss value.

To minimize the loss value, we will try to optimize the weights accordingly, by taking a derivate of the loss function to the previous weights, as shown in Figure 3-6.

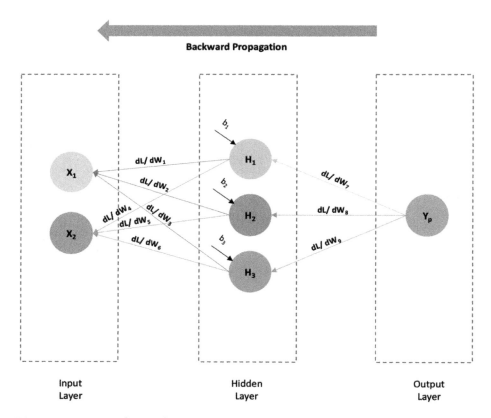

Figure 3-6. *Backward propagation*

For example, if we have to find the rate of change of loss function as compared to W_7, we would take a derivate of the Loss function to that of W_7 (dL/dW_7), and so on. As we can see from the preceding diagram, the process of taking the derivates is moving in a backward direction, that is, a backward propagation is occurring. There are multiple optimizers available to perform backward propagation, such as stochastic gradient descent (SGD), AdaGrad, among others.

Building Neural Networks with TensorFlow 2.0

Using the Keras API with TensorFlow, we will be building a simple neural network with only one hidden layer.

About the Data Set

Let's implement a simple neural network, using TensorFlow 2.0. For this, we will make use of the Fashion-MNIST data set by Zalando (The MIT License [MIT] Copyright © [2017] Zalando SE, https://tech.zalando.com), which contains 70,000 images (in grayscale) in 10 different categories. The images are 28 × 28 pixels of individual articles of clothing, with values ranging from 0 to 255, as shown in Figure 3-7.

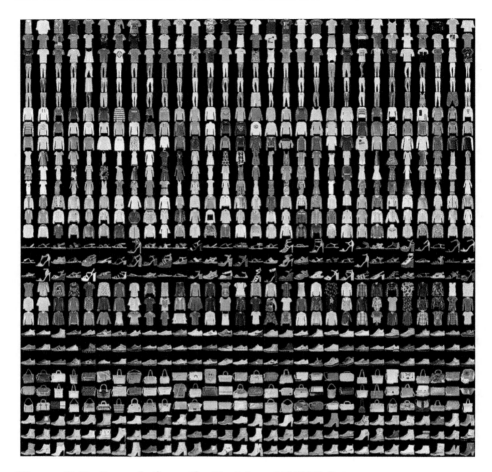

Figure 3-7. Sample from the Fashion-MNIST data set
(Source: https://bit.ly/2xqIwCH)

Of the total 70,000 images, 60,000 are used for training, and the remaining 10,000 images are used for testing. The labels are integer arrays ranging from 0 to 9. The class names are not part of the data set; therefore, we must include the following mapping for training/prediction:

Label	Description
0	T-shirt/top
1	Trouser
2	Pullover
3	Dress
4	Coat
5	Sandal
6	Shirt
7	Sneaker
8	Bag
9	Ankle boot

(Source: https://bit.ly/2xqIwCH)

Let's start by loading the necessary modules, as follows:

```
[In]: from __future__ import absolute_import, division, print_
      function, unicode_literals
[In]: import numpy as np
[In]: import tensorflow as tf
[In]: from tensorflow import keras as ks
[In]: print(tf.__version__)
[Out]: 2.0.0-rc1
```

Now, load the Fashion-MNIST data set.

```
[In]: (training_images, training_labels), (test_images, test_
      labels) = ks.datasets.fashion_mnist.load_data()
```

63

Let's undertake a little bit of data exploration, as follows:

```
[In]: print('Training Images Dataset Shape: {}'.
      format(training_images.shape))
[In]: print('No. of Training Images Dataset Labels: {}'.
      format(len(training_labels)))
[In]: print('Test Images Dataset Shape: {}'.format(test_images.
      shape))
[In]: print('No. of Test Images Dataset Labels: {}'.
      format(len(test_labels)))
[Out]: Training Images Dataset Shape: (60000, 28, 28)
[Out]: No. of Training Images Dataset Labels: 60000
[Out]: Test Images Dataset Shape: (10000, 28, 28)
[Out]: No. of Test Images Dataset Labels: 10000
```

As the pixel values range from 0 to 255, we have to rescale these values in the range 0 to 1 before pushing them to the model. We can scale these values (both for training and test data sets) by dividing the values by 255.

```
[In]: training_images = training_images / 255.0
[In]: test_images = test_images / 255.0
```

We will be using the Keras implementation to build the different layers of a neural network. We will keep it simple by having only one hidden layer.

```
[In]: input_data_shape = (28, 28)
[In]: hidden_activation_function = 'relu'
[In]: output_activation_function = 'softmax'

[In]: nn_model = models.Sequential()
[In]: nn_model.add(ks.layers.Flatten(input_shape=input_data_
      shape, name='Input_layer'))
[In]: nn_model.add(ks.layers.Dense(32, activation=hidden_
      activation_function, name='Hidden_layer'))
```

```
[In]: nn_model.add(ks.layers.Dense(10, activation=output_
      activation_function, name='Output_layer'))
[In]: nn_model.summary()
[Out]:
```

```
Model: "sequential"
```

Layer (type)	Output Shape	Param #
Input_layer (Flatten)	(None, 784)	0
Hidden_layer (Dense)	(None, 32)	25120
Output_layer (Dense)	(None, 10)	330

```
Total params: 25,450
Trainable params: 25,450
Non-trainable params: 0
```

Now, we will use an optimization function with the help of the compile method. An Adam optimizer with the objective function sparse_categorical_crossentropy, which optimizes for the accuracy metric, can be built as follows:

```
[In]: optimizer = 'adam'
[In]: loss_function = 'sparse_categorical_crossentropy'
[In]: metric = ['accuracy']
[In]: nn_model.compile(optimizer=optimizer, loss=loss_function,
      metrics=metric)
[In]: nn_model.fit(training_images, training_labels, epochs=10)
[Out]:
```

```
Train on 60000 samples
Epoch 1/10
WARNING:tensorflow:Entity <function Function._initialize_uninitialized_variables.<locals>.initia
WARNING: Entity <function Function._initialize_uninitialized_variables.<locals>.initialize_varia
60000/60000 [==============================] - 4s 74us/sample - loss: 0.5423 - accuracy: 0.8123
Epoch 2/10
60000/60000 [==============================] - 4s 58us/sample - loss: 0.4147 - accuracy: 0.8539
Epoch 3/10
60000/60000 [==============================] - 4s 60us/sample - loss: 0.3831 - accuracy: 0.8630
Epoch 4/10
60000/60000 [==============================] - 4s 59us/sample - loss: 0.3604 - accuracy: 0.8706
Epoch 5/10
60000/60000 [==============================] - 4s 59us/sample - loss: 0.3439 - accuracy: 0.8757
Epoch 6/10
60000/60000 [==============================] - 4s 59us/sample - loss: 0.3306 - accuracy: 0.8798
Epoch 7/10
60000/60000 [==============================] - 4s 60us/sample - loss: 0.3204 - accuracy: 0.8833
Epoch 8/10
60000/60000 [==============================] - 4s 59us/sample - loss: 0.3137 - accuracy: 0.8861
Epoch 9/10
60000/60000 [==============================] - 4s 60us/sample - loss: 0.3069 - accuracy: 0.8878
Epoch 10/10
60000/60000 [==============================] - 4s 60us/sample - loss: 0.2994 - accuracy: 0.8897
<tensorflow.python.keras.callbacks.History at 0x7f359adce128>
```

Following is the model evaluation:

1. Training evaluation

```
[In]: training_loss, training_accuracy = nn_model.
      evaluate(training_images, training_labels)
[In]: print('Training Data Accuracy {}'.
      format(round(float(training_accuracy),2)))
[Out]:
```

```
60000/1 [==================
Training Data Accuracy 0.9
```

2. Test evaluation

```
[In]: test_loss, test_accuracy = nn_model.evaluate(test_images,
      test_labels)
[In]: print('Test Data Accuracy {}'.format(round(float(test_
      accuracy),2))) [Out]:
```

```
10000/1 [==============:
Test Data Accuracy 0.87
```

The code for the simple neural network implementation using TensorFlow 2.0 can be found at `http://bit.ly/NNetTF2`. You can save a copy of the code and run it in the Google Colab environment. Try experimenting with different parameters and note the results.

Deep Neural Networks (DNNs)

When a simple neural network has more than one hidden layer, it is known as a deep neural network (DNN). Figure 3-8 shows the architecture of a typical DNN.

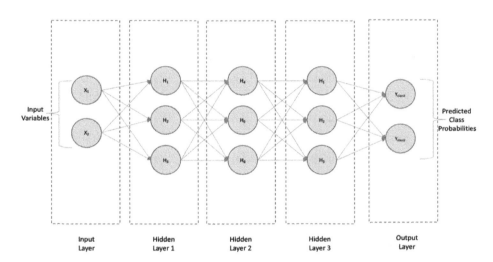

Figure 3-8. *Deep neural network with three hidden layers*

It consists of an input layer with two input variables, three hidden layers with three neurons each, and an output layer (consisting either of a single output for regression or multiple outputs for classification). The more hidden layers, the more neurons. Hence, the neural network is able to learn the nonlinear (non-convex) relation between the inputs and output. However, having more hidden layers adds to the computation cost, so one has to think in terms of a trade-off between computation cost and accuracy.

Building DNNs with TensorFlow 2.0

We will be using the Keras implementation to build a DNN with three hidden layers. The steps in the previous implementation of a simple neural network, up to the scaling part, is same for building the DNN. Therefore, we will skip those steps and start directly with building the input and hidden and output layers of the DNN, as follows:

```
[In]: input_data_shape = (28, 28)
[In]: hidden_activation_function = 'relu'
[In]: output_activation_function = 'softmax'
[In]: dnn_model = models.Sequential()
[In]: dnn_model.add(ks.layers.Flatten(input_shape=input_data_
      shape, name='Input_layer'))
[In]: dnn_model.add(ks.layers.Dense(256, activation=hidden_
      activation_function, name='Hidden_layer_1'))
[In]: dnn_model.add(ks.layers.Dense(192, activation=hidden_
      activation_function, name='Hidden_layer_2'))
[In]: dnn_model.add(ks.layers.Dense(128, activation=hidden_
      activation_function, name='Hidden_layer_3'))
[In]: dnn_model.add(ks.layers.Dense(10, activation=output_
      activation_function, name='Output_layer'))
[In]: dnn_model.summary()
[Out]:
```

```
Model: "sequential_1"
```

Layer (type)	Output Shape	Param #
Input_layer (Flatten)	(None, 784)	0
Hidden_layer_1 (Dense)	(None, 256)	200960
Hidden_layer_2 (Dense)	(None, 192)	49344
Hidden_layer_3 (Dense)	(None, 128)	24704
Output_layer (Dense)	(None, 10)	1290

```
Total params: 276,298
Trainable params: 276,298
Non-trainable params: 0
```

Now, we will use an optimization function with the help of the compile method. An Adam optimizer with the objective function sparse_categorical_crossentropy, which optimizes for the accuracy metric, can be built as follows:

```
[In]: optimizer = 'adam'
[In]: loss_function = 'sparse_categorical_crossentropy'
       metric = ['accuracy']
[In]: dnn_model.compile(optimizer=optimizer, loss=loss_
       function, metrics=metric)
[In]: dnn_model.fit(training_images, training_labels, epochs=20)
[Out]:
```

```
Train on 60000 samples
Epoch 1/20
WARNING:tensorflow:Entity <function Function._initialize_uninitialized_variables.<locals>.initiali
WARNING: Entity <function Function._initialize_uninitialized_variables.<locals>.initialize_variabl
60000/60000 [==============================] - 10s 163us/sample - loss: 0.4802 - accuracy: 0.8261
Epoch 2/20
60000/60000 [==============================] - 9s 151us/sample - loss: 0.3640 - accuracy: 0.8648
Epoch 3/20
60000/60000 [==============================] - 9s 151us/sample - loss: 0.3328 - accuracy: 0.8765
Epoch 4/20
60000/60000 [==============================] - 9s 153us/sample - loss: 0.3025 - accuracy: 0.8881
Epoch 5/20
60000/60000 [==============================] - 10s 162us/sample - loss: 0.2867 - accuracy: 0.8922
Epoch 6/20
60000/60000 [==============================] - 9s 158us/sample - loss: 0.2721 - accuracy: 0.8974
Epoch 7/20
60000/60000 [==============================] - 9s 157us/sample - loss: 0.2599 - accuracy: 0.9023
Epoch 8/20
60000/60000 [==============================] - 10s 166us/sample - loss: 0.2486 - accuracy: 0.9057
Epoch 9/20
60000/60000 [==============================] - 10s 163us/sample - loss: 0.2396 - accuracy: 0.9090
Epoch 10/20
60000/60000 [==============================] - 10s 165us/sample - loss: 0.2292 - accuracy: 0.9119
Epoch 11/20
60000/60000 [==============================] - 10s 169us/sample - loss: 0.2195 - accuracy: 0.9170
Epoch 12/20
60000/60000 [==============================] - 10s 166us/sample - loss: 0.2129 - accuracy: 0.9186
Epoch 13/20
60000/60000 [==============================] - 10s 164us/sample - loss: 0.2056 - accuracy: 0.9205
Epoch 14/20
60000/60000 [==============================] - 10s 162us/sample - loss: 0.1996 - accuracy: 0.9239
Epoch 15/20
60000/60000 [==============================] - 10s 167us/sample - loss: 0.1907 - accuracy: 0.9273
Epoch 16/20
60000/60000 [==============================] - 10s 163us/sample - loss: 0.1874 - accuracy: 0.9277
Epoch 17/20
60000/60000 [==============================] - 10s 167us/sample - loss: 0.1807 - accuracy: 0.9307
Epoch 18/20
60000/60000 [==============================] - 10s 166us/sample - loss: 0.1768 - accuracy: 0.9323
Epoch 19/20
60000/60000 [==============================] - 10s 163us/sample - loss: 0.1719 - accuracy: 0.9342
Epoch 20/20
60000/60000 [==============================] - 10s 161us/sample - loss: 0.1660 - accuracy: 0.9373
<tensorflow.python.keras.callbacks.History at 0x7f300d5db160>
```

Following is the model evaluation:

1. Training valuation

```
[In]: training_loss, training_accuracy = dnn_model.
      evaluate(training_images, training_labels)
[In]: print('Training Data Accuracy {}'.
      format(round(float(training_accuracy),2)))
[Out]:
```

```
60000/1 [====================
Training Data Accuracy 0.94
```

2. Test evaluation

```
[In]: test_loss, test_accuracy = dnn_model.evaluate(test_
      images, test_labels)
[In]: print('Test Data Accuracy {}'.format(round(float(test_
      accuracy),2)))
[Out]:
```

```
10000/1 [===============:
Test Data Accuracy 0.89
```

The code for the DNN implementation using TensorFlow 2.0 can be found at http://bit.ly/DNNTF2. You can save a copy of the code and run it in the Google Colab environment. Try experimenting with different parameters and note the results.

As observed, the training accuracy for the simple neural network is about 90%, whereas it is 94% for the DNNs, and the test accuracy for the simple neural network is about 87%, whereas it is 89% for DNNs. It goes to show that we were able to achieve higher accuracy by adding more hidden layers to the neural network architecture.

Estimators Using the Keras Model

In Chapter 2, we built various machine learning models, using premade estimators. However, the TensorFlow API also provides enough flexibility for us to build custom estimators. In this section, you will see how we can create a custom estimator, using a Keras model. The implementation follows.

Let's start by loading the necessary modules.

```
[In]: from __future__ import absolute_import, division, print_
      function, unicode_literals
[In]: import numpy as np
[In]: import pandas as pd
```

```
[In]: import tensorflow as tf
[In]: from tensorflow import keras as ks
[In]: import tensorflow_datasets as tf_ds
[In]: print(tf.__version__)
[Out]: 2.0.0-rc1
```

Now, create a function to load the iris data set.

```
[In]: def data_input():
          train_test_split = tf_ds.Split.TRAIN
          iris_dataset = tf_ds.load('iris', split=train_test_
          split, as_supervised=True)
          iris_dataset = iris_dataset.map(lambda features,
          labels: ({'dense_input':features}, labels))
          iris_dataset = iris_dataset.batch(32).repeat()
          return iris_dataset
```

Build a simple Keras model.

```
[In]: activation_function = 'relu'
[In]: input_shape = (4,)
[In]: dropout = 0.2
[In]: output_activation_function = 'sigmoid'
[In]: keras_model = ks.models.Sequential([ks.layers.Dense(16,
      activation=activation_function, input_shape=input_
      shape), ks.layers.Dropout(dropout), ks.layers.Dense(1,
      activation=output_activation_function)])
```

Now, we will use an optimization function with the help of the compile method. An Adam optimizer with the loss function categorical_ crossentropy can be built as follows:

```
[In]: loss_function = 'categorical_crossentropy'
[In]: optimizer = 'adam'
[In]: keras_model.compile(loss=loss_function, optimizer=optimizer)
```

```
[In]: keras_model.summary()
[Out]:
```

Model: "sequential"

Layer (type)	Output Shape	Param #
dense (Dense)	(None, 16)	80
dropout (Dropout)	(None, 16)	0
dense_1 (Dense)	(None, 1)	17

Total params: 97
Trainable params: 97
Non-trainable params: 0

Build the estimator, using tf.keras.estimator.model_to_estimator:

```
[In]: model_path = "/keras_estimator/"
[In]: estimator_keras_model = ks.estimator.model_to_
      estimator(keras_model=keras_model, model_dir=model_path)
```

Train and evaluate the model.

```
[In]: estimator_keras_model.train(input_fn=data_input, steps=25)
[In]: evaluation_result = estimator_keras_model.evaluate(input_
      fn=data_input, steps=10)
[In]: print('Final evaluation result: {}'.format(evaluation_result))
[Out]:
```

```
INFO:tensorflow:Evaluation [1/10]
INFO:tensorflow:Evaluation [1/10]
INFO:tensorflow:Evaluation [2/10]
INFO:tensorflow:Evaluation [2/10]
INFO:tensorflow:Evaluation [3/10]
INFO:tensorflow:Evaluation [3/10]
INFO:tensorflow:Evaluation [4/10]
INFO:tensorflow:Evaluation [4/10]
INFO:tensorflow:Evaluation [5/10]
INFO:tensorflow:Evaluation [5/10]
INFO:tensorflow:Evaluation [6/10]
INFO:tensorflow:Evaluation [6/10]
INFO:tensorflow:Evaluation [7/10]
INFO:tensorflow:Evaluation [7/10]
INFO:tensorflow:Evaluation [8/10]
INFO:tensorflow:Evaluation [8/10]
INFO:tensorflow:Evaluation [9/10]
INFO:tensorflow:Evaluation [9/10]
INFO:tensorflow:Evaluation [10/10]
INFO:tensorflow:Evaluation [10/10]
INFO:tensorflow:Finished evaluation at 2019-09-24-19:50:17
INFO:tensorflow:Finished evaluation at 2019-09-24-19:50:17
INFO:tensorflow:Saving dict for global step 25: global_step = 25, loss = 107.93587
INFO:tensorflow:Saving dict for global step 25: global_step = 25, loss = 107.93587
INFO:tensorflow:Saving 'checkpoint_path' summary for global step 25: /keras_estimator/model.ckpt-25
INFO:tensorflow:Saving 'checkpoint_path' summary for global step 25: /keras_estimator/model.ckpt-25
Fianl evaluation result: {'loss': 107.93587, 'global_step': 25}
```

The code for the DNN implementation using TensorFlow 2.0 can be found at http://bit.ly/KerasEstTF2. You can save a copy of the code and run it in the Google Colab environment. Try experimenting with different parameters and note the results.

Conclusion

In this chapter, you have seen how easy it is to build neural networks in TensorFlow 2.0 and also how to leverage Keras models, to build custom TensorFlow estimators.

CHAPTER 4

Images with TensorFlow

This chapter focuses on how we can leverage TensorFlow 2.0 for computer vision. There has been much breakthrough research and development in the field of computer vision, thanks to deep learning. In this chapter, we will start with a brief overview of image processing and move on to one of the most successful algorithms in computer vision, the convolutional neural networks (CNNs), or ConvNets. We will approach CNNs with an introduction and explain their basic architecture with a simple example. Later in this chapter, we will implement a CNN, using TensorFlow 2.0. We will move on to discuss generative networks, which are networks developed for generating images with machines. We will cover autoencoders and variational autoencoders (VAEs), which are a form of generative network. Next, we will implement VAEs, using TensorFlow 2.0, and generate some new images. In the final section, we will discuss the concept of transfer learning—how it has been leveraged in computer vision and the difference between a typical machine learning process and transfer learning. Finally, we discuss applications and the advantages of transfer learning.

© Pramod Singh, Avinash Manure 2020
P. Singh and A. Manure, *Learn TensorFlow 2.0*,
https://doi.org/10.1007/978-1-4842-5558-2_4

Image Processing

There has been much groundbreaking research conducted in the field of computer vision, primarily in the areas of object detection, recognition, and segmentation, from the 1960s to 2000s. This work was partly divided into two categories: one focused on techniques to perform image recognition, which started in the 1960s, and the other, which started after 2000, focused on collecting images data as a benchmark to evaluate the techniques.

Some notable research related to image recognition techniques included "Blocks World," by Larry Roberts, in 1963, which is considered to be the first Ph.D. dissertation in computer vision. In it, the visual world was simplified into simple geometric shapes, the goal being to recognize and reconstruct them.

Work in the area of collecting images data for benchmarking began in the year 2006, starting with the PASCAL Visual Object Classes challenge, which had a data set of 20 object categories and was composed of several thousand to about 10,000 labeled objects per category. Many groups started using this data set to test their techniques, and, thus, a new paradigm shift occurred. About the same time, a group of scholars at Princeton and Stanford Universities began to consider whether we were ready to recognize most objects or all objects, which led to a project called ImageNet. This is a collection of 14M+ images spread over 22K categories. It was the biggest artificial intelligence (AI)-related data set at the time. The ImageNet Large Scale Visual Recognition Challenge resulted in many groundbreaking algorithms, one of which was AlexNet (CNN), which beat all other algorithms, to win the ImageNet challenge in 2012.

Convolutional Neural Networks

Convolutional neural networks, abbreviated as CNNs or ConvNets, are a special class of neural networks that specializes in processing grid-like topology data, such as images. They consist of three distinct layers:

- Convolutional

- Pooling

- Fully connected

Convolutional Layer

In a CNN, a convolutional layer is essentially responsible for applying one or more filters to an input. This is the layer that distinguishes convolutional neural networks from other neural networks. Each convolutional layer contains one or more filters, known as convolutional kernels. A filter is basically a matrix of integers that is used on a subset of the input image, which is of the same size as the filter. Each pixel from the subset is multiplied by the corresponding value in the kernel, and then the result is summed up for a single value. This is repeated until the filter "slides" across the whole image, thus creating an output feature map. The magnitude of movement between applications of the filter to the input image is referred to as the stride, and it is almost always symmetrical in height and width.

For example, suppose we have a grayscale image of 9×9 pixels that has one channel (a 2D matrix) and a 3×3 convolutional kernel. If we choose a stride of $(1,1)$, i.e., sliding the kernel by 1 pixel horizontally and 1 pixel vertically over the whole of the image, we get an output feature map of 7×7.

-1	-1	-1	-1	-1	-1	-1	-1	-1
-1	1	-1	-1	-1	-1	-1	1	-1
-1	-1	1	-1	-1	-1	1	-1	-1
-1	-1	-1	1	-1	1	-1	-1	-1
-1	-1	-1	-1	1	-1	-1	-1	-1
-1	-1	-1	1	-1	1	-1	-1	-1
-1	-1	1	-1	-1	-1	1	-1	-1
-1	1	-1	-1	-1	-1	-1	1	-1
-1	-1	-1	-1	-1	-1	-1	-1	-1

Input grayscale image of letter X (9 × 9 pixels)

1	-1	-1
-1	1	-1
-1	-1	1

Convolutional kernel (3 × 3 pixels)

-1 (x1)	-1 (x-1)	-1 (x-1)	-1	-1	-1	-1	-1	-1
-1 (x-1)	1 (x1)	-1 (x-1)	-1	-1	-1	-1	1	-1
-1 (x-1)	-1 (x-1)	1 (x1)	-1	-1	-1	1	-1	-1
-1	-1	-1	1	-1	1	-1	-1	-1
-1	-1	-1	-1	1	-1	-1	-1	-1
-1	-1	-1	1	-1	1	-1	-1	-1
-1	-1	1	-1	-1	-1	1	-1	-1
-1	1	-1	-1	-1	-1	-1	1	-1
-1	-1	-1	-1	-1	-1	-1	-1	-1

First dot product of subset of input image with kernel

-1	-1 (x1)	-1 (x-1)	-1 (x-1)	-1	-1	-1	-1	-1
-1	1 (x-1)	-1 (x1)	-1 (x-1)	-1	-1	-1	1	-1
-1	-1 (x-1)	1 (x-1)	-1 (x1)	-1	-1	1	-1	-1
-1	-1	-1	1	-1	1	-1	-1	-1
-1	-1	-1	-1	1	-1	-1	-1	-1
-1	-1	-1	1	-1	1	-1	-1	-1
-1	-1	1	-1	-1	-1	1	-1	-1
-1	1	-1	-1	-1	-1	-1	1	-1
-1	-1	-1	-1	-1	-1	-1	-1	-1

Second dot product of subset of input image with kernel (stride (1,1))

0.77	-0.11	0.11	0.33	0.55	-0.11	0.33
-0.11	1	-0.11	0.33	-0.11	0.11	-0.11
0.11	-0.11	1	-0.33	0.11	-0.11	0.55
0.33	0.33	-0.33	0.55	-0.33	0.33	0.33
0.55	-0.11	0.11	-0.33	1	-0.11	0.11
-0.11	0.11	-0.11	0.33	-0.11	1	-0.11
0.33	-0.11	0.55	0.33	0.11	-0.11	0.77

Final feature map of 7 × 7 after kernel strides through whole input image

Usually, for the final feature output, an activation function (e.g., ReLU [rectified linear unit]) is applied. ReLU basically ensures that there is no negative value in the feature output matrix, by forcing these (negative values) to zero (Figure 4-1).

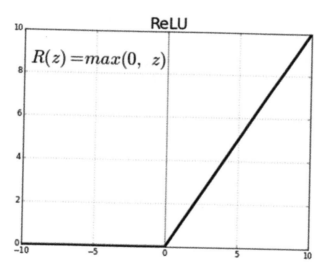

Figure 4-1. *ReLU function*

0.77	0	0.11	0.33	0.55	0	0.33
0	1	0	0.33	0	0.11	0
0.11	0	1	0	0.11	0	0.55
0.33	0.33	0	0.55	0	0.33	0.33
0.55	0	0.11	0	1	0	0.11
0	0.11	0	0.33	0	1	0
0.33	0	0.55	0.33	0.11	0	0.77

Output of ReLU function

Pooling Layer

Pooling layers help to reduce the dimensionality of the input features, thus reducing the total number of parameters and complexity of the model. One of the most widely used pooling techniques is max pooling. As the name implies, this technique takes only the maximum from a pool. As an example, let us perform pooling with a window size 2 and a stride 2 on the output of the ReLU that we derived previously.

0.77	0	0.11	0.33	0.55	0	0.33
0	1	0	0.33	0	0.11	0
0.11	0	1	0	0.11	0	0.55
0.33	0.33	0	0.55	0	0.33	0.33
0.55	0	0.11	0	1	0	0.11
0	0.11	0	0.33	0	1	0
0.33	0	0.55	0.33	0.11	0	0.77

In this case, we take the maximum of (0.77, 0, 0, 1.0), i.e., 1.0 from the first pool.

0.77	0	0.11	0.33	0.55	0	0.33
0	1	0	0.33	0	0.11	0
0.11	0	1	0	0.11	0	0.55
0.33	0.33	0	0.55	0	0.33	0.33
0.55	0	0.11	0	1	0	0.11
0	0.11	0	0.33	0	1	0
0.33	0	0.55	0.33	0.11	0	0.77

We take the maximum of (0.11, 0.33, 0, 0.33), i.e., 0.33 from the second pool.

Finally, when we have made all the strides, we get the following output:

1	0.33	0.55	0.33
0.33	1	0.33	0.55
0.55	0.33	1	0.11
0.33	0.55	0.11	0.77

Fully Connected Layer

This layer is the same as any artificial neural network (ANN) system in which the neurons have complete connection to all the activations from the previous layers (Figure 4-2).

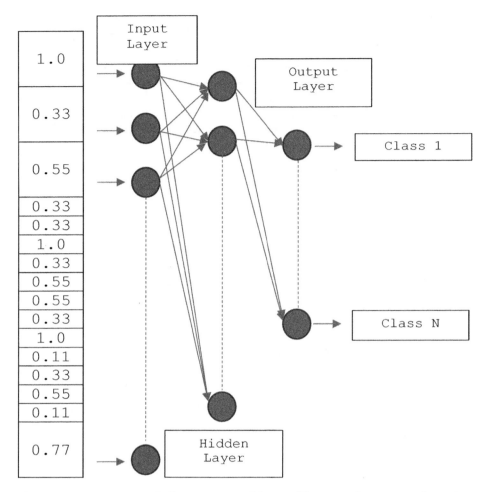

Figure 4-2. *Input to fully connected layer (flattened output of pooling layer)*

ConvNets Using TensorFlow 2.0

Let us implement a simple convolutional neural network using TensorFlow 2.0. For this, we will make use of the Fashion-MNIST data set by Zalando (The MIT License [MIT] Copyright © [2017] Zalando SE, https://tech.zalando.com), which contains 70,000 images (in grayscale) in 10 different categories. The images are 28 × 28 pixels of individual articles of clothing, with values ranging from 0 to 255, as shown in Figure 4-3.

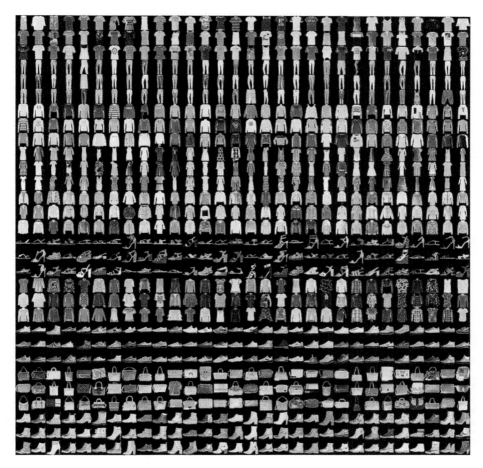

Figure 4-3. *Images from the Fashion-MNIST data set by Zalando (Source: https://bit.ly/2xqIwCH)*

Of the total 70,000 images, 60,000 are used for training and the remaining 10,000 for testing. The labels are integer arrays ranging from 0 to 9. The class names are not a part of the data set. Therefore, we must include the following mapping for training/prediction:

Label	Description
0	T-shirt/top
1	Trouser
2	Pullover
3	Dress
4	Coat
5	Sandal
6	Shirt
7	Sneaker
8	Bag
9	Ankle boot

(Source: https://bit.ly/2xqIwCH*)*

Let's start by loading the necessary modules.

```
[In]: from __future__ import absolute_import, division,
      print_function, unicode_literals
[In]: import numpy as np
[In]: import tensorflow as tf
[In]: from tensorflow import keras as ks
[In]: print(tf.__version__)
[Out]: 2.0.0-rc1
```

Now, load the Fashion-MNIST data set.

```
[In]: mnist_fashion = ks.datasets.fashion_mnist
[In]: (training_images, training_labels), (test_images,
      test_labels) = mnist_fashion.load_data()
```

Let's undertake a little bit of data exploration.

```
[In]: print('Training Dataset Shape: {}'.format(training_
       images.shape))
[In]: print('No. of Training Dataset Labels: {}'.
       format(len(training_labels)))
[In]: print('Test Dataset Shape: {}'.format(test_images.shape))
[In]: print('No. of Test Dataset Labels: {}'.format(len(test_
       labels)))
[Out]: Training Dataset Shape: (60000, 28, 28)
[Out]: No. of Training Dataset Labels: 60000
[Out]: Test Dataset Shape: (10000, 28, 28)
[Out]: No. of Test Dataset Labels: 10000
```

As the pixel values range from 0 to 255, we will scale those values in the range of 0 to 1 before pushing them to the model. We can scale these values (both for training and test data sets) by dividing the values by 255.

```
[In]: training_images = training_images / 255.0
[In]: test_images = test_images / 255.0
```

We can reshape the training and test data set by reshaping the matrices into a $28 \times 28 \times 1$ array, as follows:

```
[In]: training_images = training_images.reshape((60000, 28, 28, 1))
[In]: test_images = test_images.reshape((10000, 28, 28, 1))

[In]: print('Training Dataset Shape: {}'.format(training_
       images.shape))
[In]: print('No. of Training Dataset Labels: {}'.
       format(len(training_labels)))
[In]: print('Test Dataset Shape: {}'.format(test_images.shape))
[In]: print('No. of Test Dataset Labels: {}'.format(len(test_
       labels)))
```

```
[Out]: Training Dataset Shape: (60000, 28, 28, 1)
[Out]: No. of Training Dataset Labels: 60000
[Out]: Test Dataset Shape: (10000, 28, 28, 1)
[Out]: No. of Test Dataset Labels: 10000
```

Now, let's build the different layers of the model. We will be using the Keras implementation to build the different layers of a CNN. We will keep it simple, by having only three layers.

> *First layer—convolutional layer with ReLU activation function*: This layer takes the 2D array (28 × 28 pixels) as input. We will take 50 convolutional kernels (filters) of shape 3 × 3 pixels. The output of which will be passed to a ReLU activation function before being passed to the next layer.

```
[In]: cnn_model = ks.models.Sequential()
[In]: cnn_model.add(ks.layers.Conv2D(50, (3, 3), activation='relu',
      input_shape=(28, 28, 1), name='Conv2D_layer'))
```

> *Second layer—pooling layer*: This layer takes the 50 26 × 26 2D arrays as input and transforms them into the same number (50) of arrays, with dimensions half that of the original (i.e., from 26 × 26 to 13 × 13 pixels).

```
[In]: cnn_model.add(ks.layers.MaxPooling2D((2, 2),
      name='Maxpooling_2D'))
```

> *Third layer—fully connected layer*: This layer takes the 50 13 × 13 2D arrays as input and transforms them into a 1D array of 8450 elements (50 × 13 × 13). These 8450 input elements are passed through a fully connected neural network that gives the probability scores for each of the 10 output labels (at the output layer).

```
[In]: cnn_model.add(ks.layers.Flatten(name='Flatten'))
[In]: cnn_model.add(ks.layers.Dense(50, activation='relu',
      name='Hidden_layer'))
[In]: cnn_model.add(ks.layers.Dense(10, activation='softmax',
      name='Output_layer'))
```

We can check the details of different layers built in the CNN model by using the summary method shown below:

```
[In]: cnn_model.summary()
[Out]:
```

```
Model: "sequential_2"
```

Layer (type)	Output Shape	Param #
Conv2D_layer (Conv2D)	(None, 26, 26, 50)	500
Maxpooling_2D (MaxPooling2D)	(None, 13, 13, 50)	0
Flatten (Flatten)	(None, 8450)	0
Hidden_layer (Dense)	(None, 50)	422550
Output_layer (Dense)	(None, 10)	510

```
Total params: 423,560
Trainable params: 423,560
Non-trainable params: 0
```

Now we will use an optimization function with the help of the compile method. An Adam optimizer with objective function sparse_categorical_crossentropy, which optimizes for the accuracy metric, can be built as follows:

```
[In]: cnn_model.compile(optimizer='adam', loss='sparse_
      categorical_crossentropy', metrics=['accuracy'])
```

Model training:

```
[In]: cnn_model.fit(training_images, training_labels, epochs=10)
[Out]:
```

```
Train on 60000 samples
Epoch 1/10
WARNING:tensorflow:Entity <function Function._initialize_uninitialized_variables.<locals>.initiali
WARNING: Entity <function Function._initialize_uninitialized_variables.<locals>.initialize_variabl
60000/60000 [==============================] - 44s 740us/sample - loss: 0.4183 - accuracy: 0.8541
Epoch 2/10
60000/60000 [==============================] - 43s 712us/sample - loss: 0.2834 - accuracy: 0.8983
Epoch 3/10
60000/60000 [==============================] - 43s 710us/sample - loss: 0.2432 - accuracy: 0.9125
Epoch 4/10
60000/60000 [==============================] - 42s 703us/sample - loss: 0.2145 - accuracy: 0.9227
Epoch 5/10
60000/60000 [==============================] - 42s 700us/sample - loss: 0.1902 - accuracy: 0.9297
Epoch 6/10
60000/60000 [==============================] - 42s 698us/sample - loss: 0.1685 - accuracy: 0.9381
Epoch 7/10
60000/60000 [==============================] - 42s 699us/sample - loss: 0.1490 - accuracy: 0.9453
Epoch 8/10
60000/60000 [==============================] - 42s 695us/sample - loss: 0.1346 - accuracy: 0.9506
Epoch 9/10
60000/60000 [==============================] - 42s 694us/sample - loss: 0.1188 - accuracy: 0.9567
Epoch 10/10
60000/60000 [==============================] - 41s 688us/sample - loss: 0.1047 - accuracy: 0.9619
<tensorflow.python.keras.callbacks.History at 0x7f48b2d8e240>
```

Model evaluation:

1. Training evaluation

    ```
    [In]: training_loss, training_accuracy = cnn_model.
          evaluate(training_images, training_labels)
    [In]: print('Training Accuracy {}'.
          format(round(float(training_accuracy), 2)))
    [Out]:
    ```

    ```
    60000/1 [===============:
    Training Accuracy 0.97
    ```

2. Test evaluation

```
[In]: test_loss, test_accuracy = cnn_model.
      evaluate(test_images, test_labels)
[In]: print('Test Accuracy {}'.format(round(float
      (test_accuracy), 2))) [Out]:


      10000/1 [=========:
      Test Accuracy 0.91
```

From the preceding evaluation, we see that we were able to achieve about 97% accuracy in the training data set and about 91% accuracy in the test data set, with only a simple CNN architecture. This goes to prove that CNNs are powerful algorithms for image recognition.

The code for the CNN implementation using TensorFlow 2.0 can be found at http://bit.ly/CNNTF2. You can save a copy of the code and run it in the Google Colab environment. Try experimenting with different parameters and note the results.

Advanced Convolutional Neural Network Architectures

CNNs have come a long way since they were first introduced in the 1990s. Let's look at some of the recent CNN-based architectures that have entered the limelight.

1. VGG-16. This convolutional neural network was introduced by K. Simonyan and A. Zisserman, from the University of Oxford, in the paper "Very Deep Convolutional Networks for Large-Scale Image

Recognition." The main difference between AlexNet and VGG-16 is that VGG-16 uses multiple 3×3 kernels as filters, instead of the large filters used in AlexNet (11 filters in the first convolutional layer, and 5 filters in the second). This led to an accuracy of 92.7%—among the top five in the ImageNet challenge—and this model was also submitted to ILSVRC-2014, at which it was the runner-up. Figure 4-4 shows a typical VGG-16 architecture.

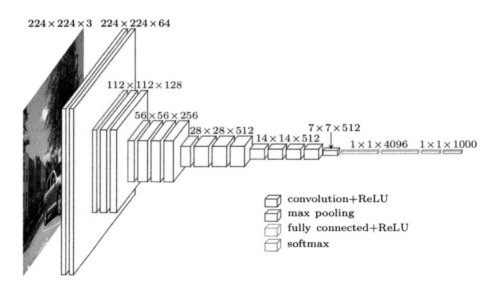

Figure 4-4. *VGG-16 architecture*

2. Inception(GoogleNet). This was developed by
    Google and was the winner of the ILSVRC-2014
    competition wherein it achieved a top-5 error rate of
    6.67%. An inception module was used with smaller
    convolutions that made possible to reduce the
    number of parameters to 4 million only. Figure 4-5
    shows the GoogleNet architecture.

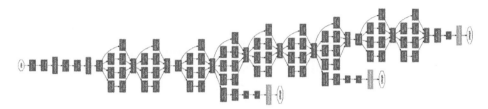

Figure 4-5. *GoogleNet architecture*

3. ResNet. This architecture was developed by Kaiming
    He, Xiangyu Zhang, Shaoqing Ren, and Jian Sun in
    2015. It won the ILSVRC-2015 competition, with a
    top-five error rate of 3.57%, which was lower than
    the human error top-five rate. Figure 4-6 shows the
    ResNet architecture.

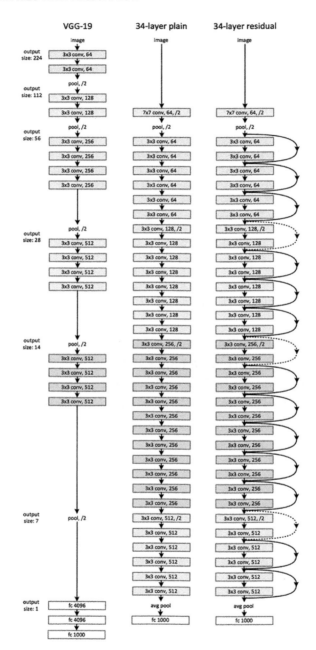

Figure 4-6. *ResNet architecture*

4. DenseNet. This architecture was developed by
    Gao Huang, Zhuang Liu, Laurens van der Maaten,
    and Kilian Q. Weinberger in 2016. DenseNet was
    reported to achieve better performance with
    less complexity, compared to ResNet. A typical
    DenseNet architecture is depicted in Figure 4-7.

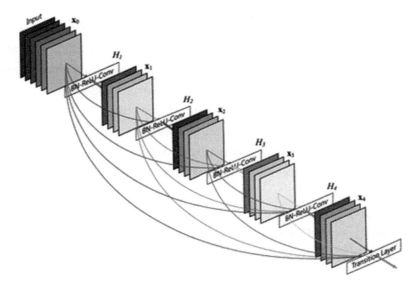

Figure 4-7. *DenseNet architecture*

Transfer Learning

Imagine that there are two friends, A and B, who recently planned to learn
to drive a car, so that once they finished learning, they could buy a car for
their commute. Suppose A used to take public transportation to commute,
and B used a geared bike. Now, when both start to learn to drive a car,
assuming that both A and B have the same intelligence level, who will
be in a better position to learn more quickly? Yes, you're right; it will be
B. Because B has been using a bike, he will be applying his knowledge of
controlling the bike, through the combination of clutch, gear, accelerator,
and brakes, to control a car. The only new skill he must learn is to adjust

his driving for a car, which is much bigger than a bike. For A, driving a car requires an entirely new skill set, as he has never ridden a bike/car. Hence, he will require more time and effort to learn to drive a car. This example illustrates how a typical human behavior acquired through past experiences of performing a certain task can be applied to a new but similar or related task. This has helped humans evolve faster and spend less time and effort on learning new tasks.

The same thing, applied to machine learning, is called transfer learning. According to the book *Deep Learning* by Ian Goodfellow, Aaron Courville, and Yoshua Bengio (MIT Press, 2016), the definition of transfer learning is a "situation where what has been learned in one setting is exploited to improve generalization in another setting."

Let's derive a mathematical formula in support of the preceding definition, using the example of learning to drive a car that was mentioned previously. Let's first understand what a *domain* and *task* are, with respect to transfer learning.

A domain $\mathbf{D}$ comprises a feature space $\mathbf{S}$ and a marginal probability distribution (mpd) $\mathbf{P(X)}$, where $\mathbf{S} = \mathbf{s_1,...,s_n} \in \mathbf{S}$. Given a specific domain, $\mathbf{D} = \{\mathbf{S}, \mathbf{P(S)}\}$, a task consists of a label space $\mathbf{Y}$ and an objective predictive function $\mathbf{f(\cdot)}$ (denoted by $\mathbf{T} = \{\mathbf{P}, \mathbf{f(\cdot)}\}$), which is not observed but can be learned from the training data, which consist of pairs $\{\mathbf{s_i}, \mathbf{p_i}\}$, where $\mathbf{s_i} \in \mathbf{S}$ and $\mathbf{p_i} \in \mathbf{P}$. The function $\mathbf{f(\cdot)}$ can be used to predict the corresponding label, $\mathbf{f(s)}$, of a new instance $\mathbf{s}$. Probabilistically, $\mathbf{f(s)}$ can be written as $\mathbf{P(p|s)}$. Let's suppose we denote the activity of riding a bike as $\mathbf{D_S}$ and call it as a source domain. Now let's call the activity of driving a car $\mathbf{D_T}$ and call it as target domain. Suppose riding a bike on a busy street is one task $\mathbf{T_S}$ of the domain $\mathbf{D_S}$, whereas driving a car on a busy street is a task $\mathbf{T_T}$ of domain $\mathbf{D_T}$.

Mathematically, given a source domain $\mathbf{D_S}$ and a learning task $\mathbf{T_S}$, a target domain $\mathbf{D_T}$ and learning task $\mathbf{T_T}$, the aim of transfer learning is to help improve the learning of the (target) predictive function $\mathbf{f_T(\cdot)}$ in $\mathbf{D_T}$, leveraging the knowledge in D_S and T_S, where $D_S \neq D_T$ or $T_S \neq T_T$. In simple terms, transfer learning is the use of knowledge gained by B in riding his bike on a busy street, applied to driving a car on another busy street.

Transfer Learning and Machine Learning

In the preceding example, if the target and source domains are the same, i.e., if driving a car is both the source as well as the target domain ($D_S = D_T$), and the learning tasks are the same or similar, i.e., driving a car in two different busy streets ($T_S = T_T$), the learning problem becomes a traditional machine learning problem. However, one should note that transfer learning is an application of a research problem to a machine learning problem and not an algorithm or technique. Transfer learning is different from traditional machine learning, as it uses pre-trained models that have been built with some task T_S as an input to be used for another task T_T in a way that will help to jump-start the development process for task T_T.

Figure 4-8 depicts a typical machine learning system. We can see that for a particular task for a given domain, the machine learning model is able to learn and generalize well. However, if there is a new task from a different domain, it must build an altogether new model, to be able to generalize for that task/domain.

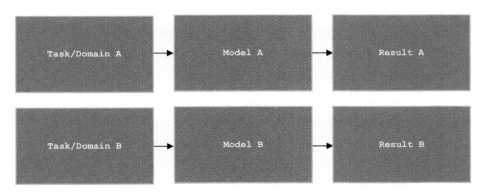

Figure 4-8. *Machine learning methodology*

95

Figure 4-9 depicts a typical transfer learning methodology. We can see that for Task/Domain A, the machine learning model is able to learn and generalize well. Now, here, we extract the "general" knowledge gained from Task/Domain A and apply it to a similar Task/Domain B.

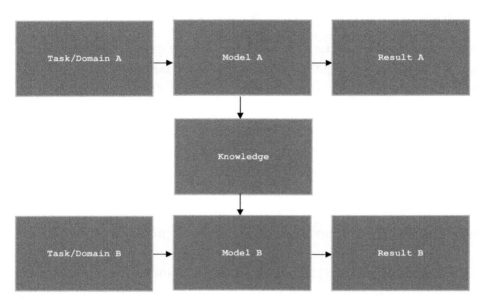

Figure 4-9. *Transfer learning methodology*

Following are applications of transfer learning:

1. Deep learning/image recognition: Use of Word2vec and fastText models for sentiment analysis of Twitter data on a particular topic

2. Natural language processing: Use of AlexNet and Inceptions models for object detection

Following are advantages of transfer learning:

1. Reduced training time, by using some of the modules of an already developed model to a new one

2. Usefulness in scenarios in which there is not sufficient data to train a model for desired results

Variational Autoencoders Using TensorFlow 2.0

To understand what variational autoencoders are, you must first understand what autoencoders are, where they are used, and what the difference is between VAEs and the other forms of autoencoders.

Autoencoders

Autoencoders are a type of ANN that is used to generate output data in the same unsupervised manner as for input data. An autoencoder essentially comprises two main parts: an encoder and a decoder. The encoder compresses the input data into a lower dimensional representation of it, and the decoder decompresses the representation into the original input data. Figure 4-10 shows a simple autoencoder applied on images.

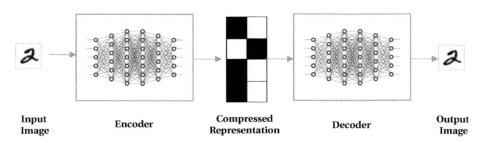

| Input Image | Encoder | Compressed Representation | Decoder | Output Image |

Figure 4-10. *Basic autoencoder*

Applications of Autoencoders

One limitation of autoencoders is that they can only be used to reconstruct data that the encoder part of the autoencoders has seen during the training. They cannot be used to generate new data. This is where variational autoencoders enter the picture.

Following are two applications of autoencoders:

1. As a dimensionality reduction technique to observe/visualize high-dimensional data into lower dimensions

2. As a compression technique to save memory and network cost

Variational Autoencoders

A VAE is a type of generative model plus general autoencoders that let us sample from the model, to generate data. Most VAE architecture is the same as that of a generic autoencoder, except that VAEs force the compressed representation of the input data to follow a zero mean and a unit variance Gaussian distribution. A simple VAE architecture is shown in Figure 4-11.

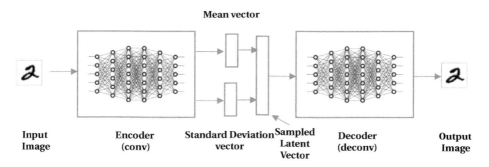

Figure 4-11. *Basic VAE architecture*

Implementation of Variational Autoencoders Using TensorFlow 2.0

Let's build a VAE model that will help us to generate new handwritten digits, using the Fashion-MNIST data set. This data set comprises 70,000 images (black-and-white) of handwritten digits, ranging from 0 to 9, out of which 60,000 are for training, and the remaining 10,000 are for testing. Each grayscale image is normalized to fit a 28 × 28 pixel bounding box.

1. Load the required Python modules.

```
[In]: import time
[In]: import PIL as pil
[In]: import numpy as np
[In]: import tensorflow as tf
[In]: from IPython import display
[In]: import matplotlib.pyplot as mpy
[In]: from tensorflow import keras as ks
[In]: from tensorflow.keras.datasets import mnist
```

2. Load the Fashion-MNIST data set with train-test split, normalization, and binarization.

```
[In]: (training_data, _), (test_data, _) = mnist.load_data()
[In]: training_data = training_data.reshape(training_data.
      shape[0], 28, 28, 1).astype('float32')
[In]: test_data = test_data.reshape(test_data.shape[0], 28,
      28, 1).astype('float32')
[In]: training_data = training_data/255.0
[In]: test_data = test_data/255.0
[In]: training_data[training_data >= 0.5] = 1.0
[In]: training_data[training_data < 0.5] = 0.0
[In]: test_data[test_data >= 0.5] = 1.0
[In]: test_data[test_data < 0.5] = 0.0
```

3. Batching and shuffling the data set

```
[In]: training_batch = tf.data.Dataset.from_tensor_
      slices(training_data).shuffle(60000).batch(50)
      test_batch = tf.data.Dataset.from_tensor_slices(test_
      data).shuffle(10000).batch(50)
```

4. Use tf.keras.Sequential to build the encoder and
    decoder.

We will be building two convolutional neural networks for the encoder
and decoder wrapping, with tf.keras.Sequential.

```
[In]: kernel_size = 3
[In]: strides_2_2 = (2, 2)
[In]: strides_1_1 = (1, 1)
[In]: activation = 'relu'
[In]: padding = 'SAME'

[In]: class CONV_VAE(ks.Model):
          #Initialization
          def __init__(self, latent_dimension):
              super(CONV_VAE, self).__init__()
              self.latent_vector = latent_vector

              #Build Encoder Model with two Convolutional Layers
              self.encoder_model = ks.Sequential(
                              [
                              ks.layers.InputLayer(input_
                              shape=(28, 28, 1)),
                              ks.layers.Conv2D
                              (filters=25, kernel_
                              size=kernel_size,
                              strides=strides_2_2,
                              activation=activation),
```

```
            ks.layers.
            Conv2D(filters=50,
            kernel_size=kernel_size,
            strides=strides_2_2,
            activation=activation),
            ks.layers.Flatten(),
            ks.layers.Dense(latent_
            vector + latent_vector),
            ]
)

        #Build Decoder Model
        self.decoder_model = ks.Sequential(
                            [
                            ks.layers.InputLayer
                            (input_shape=(latent_
                            vector,)),
                            ks.layers.
                            Dense(units=7*7*25,
                            activation=activation),
                            ks.layers.Reshape(target_
                            shape=(7, 7, 25)),
                            ks.layers.Conv2DTranspose
                            (filters=50, kernel_
                            size=kernel_size,
                            strides=strides_2_2,
                            padding=padding,
                            activation=activation),
```

```
                              ks.layers.Conv2DTranspose
                              (filters=25, kernel_
                              size=kernel_size,
                              strides=strides_2_2,
                              padding=padding,
                              activation=activation),
                              ks.layers.
                              Conv2DTranspose(filters=1,
                              kernel_size=kernel_size,
                              strides=strides_1_1,
                              padding=padding),
                              ]
)

    @tf.function
    #Sampling Function for taking samples out of encoder
    output
    def sampling(self, sam=None):
        if sam is None:
            sam = tf.random.normal(shape=(50, self.
            latent_vector))
            return self.decoder(sam, apply_sigmoid=True)

    #Encoder Function
    def encoder(self, inp):
        mean, logd = tf.split(self.encoder_model(inp),
        num_or_size_splits=2, axis=1)
        return mean, logd

    #Reparameterization Function
    def reparameterization(self, mean, logd):
        sam = tf.random.normal(shape=mean.shape)
        return sam * tf.exp(logd * 0.5) + mean
```

```
#Decoder Function
def decoder(self, out, apply_sigmoid=False):
    logout = self.decoder_model(out)
    if apply_sigmoid:
        probabs = tf.sigmoid(logout)
        return probabs

    return logout
```

5. Build an optimizer function.

```
[In]: optimizer_func = tf.keras.optimizers.Adam(0.0001)
      def log_normal_prob_dist_func(sampling, mean_value, logd,
      raxis=1):
          log_2_pi = tf.math.log(2.0 * np.pi)
          return tf.reduce_sum(-0.5 * ((sampling - mean_
          value) ** 2.0 * tf.exp(-logd) + logd + log_2_pi),
          axis=raxis)

      @tf.function
      def loss_func(model_object, inp):
          mean_value, logd = model_object.encoder(inp)
          out = model_object.reparameterization(mean_value, logd)
          log_inp = model_object.decoder(out)
          cross_entropy = tf.nn.sigmoid_cross_entropy_with_
          logits(logits=log_inp, labels=inp)
          logp_inp_out = -tf.reduce_sum(cross_entropy,
          axis=[1, 2, 3])
          logp_out = log_normal_prob_dist_func(out, 0.0, 0.0)
          logq_out_inp = log_normal_prob_dist_func(out, mean_
          value, logd)
          return -tf.reduce_mean(logp_inp_out + logp_out -
          logq_out_inp)
```

```
@tf.function
def gradient_func(model_object, inp, optimizer_func):
    with tf.GradientTape() as tape:
        loss = loss_func(vae_model, inp)
    gradients = tape.gradient(loss, model_object.
    trainable_variables)
    optimizer_func.apply_gradients(zip(gradients, model_
    object.trainable_variables))
```

6. Training

```
[In]: epochs = 100
[In]: latent_vector = 8
[In]: examples = 8
[In]: rand_vec = tf.random.normal(shape=[examples, latent_vector])
[In]: vae_model = CONV_VAE(latent_vector)
```

7. Generate an image with a trained model.

```
[In]: def generate_and_save_images(vae_model, epochs,
input_data):
        preds = vae_model.sampling(input_data)
        fig = mpy.figure(figsize=(4,4))
        for i in range(preds.shape[0]):
            mpy.subplot(4, 4, i+1)
            mpy.imshow(preds[i, :, :, 0], cmap='gray')
            mpy.axis('off')

        mpy.savefig('img_at_epoch{:04d}.png'.format(epochs))
        mpy.show()
[In]: generate_and_save_images(vae_model, 0, rand_vec)
[In]: for epoch in range(1, epochs + 1):
        start_time = time.time()
```

```
for x in training_batch:
    gradient_func(vae_model, x, optimizer_func)
end_time = time.time()
if epoch % 1 == 0:
    loss = ks.metrics.Mean()
    for y in test_batch:
        loss(loss_func(vae_model, y))
    elbo = -loss.result()
    display.clear_output(wait=False)
    print('Epoch no.: {}, Test batch ELBO: {}, '
'elapsed time for current epoch {}'.format(epochs,
elbo, end_time - start_time))
    generate_and_save_images(vae_model, epochs,
    rand_vec)
```
[Out]:

Epoch no.: 100, Test batch ELBO: -94.16806030273438, elapsed time for current epoch 6.545580148696899

As we can see from the preceding, we were able to generate new images of handwritten digits, using the Fashion-MNIST data set for training.

The code for the VAE implementation using TensorFlow 2.0 can be found at http://bit.ly/CNNVAETF2. You can save a copy of the code and run it in the Google Colab environment. Try experimenting with different parameters and note the results.

Conclusion

In this chapter, we have explored various well-known architectures for image processing and generation. Also, we have considered the concept of transfer learning and how it has helped to speed up machine learning development and bring more accuracy to models for which training data is not abundant. Finally, you have seen how we can leverage the TensorFlow and Keras APIs, to build these architectures.

CHAPTER 5

Natural Language Processing with TensorFlow 2.0

This chapter focuses on some of the aspects of natural language processing (NLP), using TensorFlow 2.0. NLP is a complex field in itself, and there are multiple tools and techniques available in the open source community for users to leverage. This chapter is mainly divided into three parts. The first offers a brief introduction to NLP and the building blocks of text processing in TensorFlow 2.0. In the second part, we discuss word embeddings and how they can be used to detect the semantic meaning of words. In the final part, we will build a deep neural network, to predict the sentiment of a user review. We will also plot word embeddings, using the TensorFlow Projector, and view them in 3D space.

NLP Overview

NLP is a vast field, and we will touch upon some fundamental shifts that have occurred over last few decades. NLP research goes back to the 1950s, when people started to work on problems related to language translation. It has evolved since then, and we are witnessing some groundbreaking work in this area of research. If we consider how this evolution has been

© Pramod Singh, Avinash Manure 2020
P. Singh and A. Manure, *Learn TensorFlow 2.0*,
https://doi.org/10.1007/978-1-4842-5558-2_5

occurring, we can consult the NLP curve chart that has been mentioned in the paper "Jumping NLP Curves" (Cambria and White, 2014), as shown in Figure 5-1.

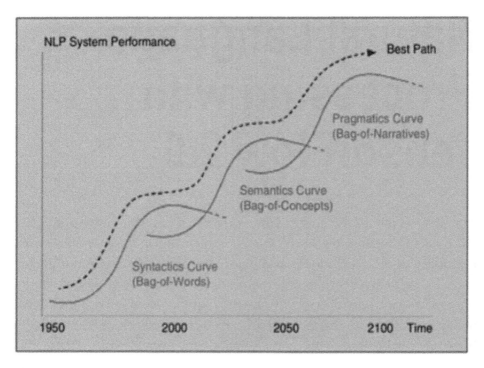

Figure 5-1. *NLP curves*

We start with the syntactic layer, where the focus is to deconstruct the text into smaller pieces. Techniques such as POS (parts of speech) tagging, chunking, and lemmatization were carried out to bring the overall text into a more desirable form. This is what is known as a "bag-of-words" approach. Slowly and gradually, we have moved into what is known as the second layer—semantics curve. In this layer, it's all about extracting the meaning of the text. It uses different techniques under the hood to figure out the concept and meaning of the words in the text. It helped to evolve from simply using text as symbols to actually using them for their meaning and relevance in the overall text. This stage is also known as "bag-of-concepts" model. The final and third phase of the NLP curve time line is the pragmatics curve, which goes beyond just the meaning of text but, rather, deals with contextual information. The ability to decode sarcasm, understand deep aspects of polarity, and personality recognition is what it strives for. Researchers are already working in this direction to reach this stage. It entails lot of components associated with text and computers. In fact, NLP is what falls at the cross section of linguistics and computers.

Text data makes up a huge percentage of the total data being generated on a global level. Therefore, it provides an incredible platform that can be used in many other ways. One of the most impactful use cases in terms of text data has been to identify the perception of the people related to a particular brand, based on the reviews they write. It has helped businesses to recalibrate their strategies to manage their brand value in the market. Supervised learning problems under the text category can be broadly identified as

- Reviews/text classification

- Text summarization (news, blogs, journals)

- Spam detection

- Audience segmentation on social media platforms

- Chatbot

In this chapter, we are going to focus on the text classification type.

Text Preprocessing

Text data can either be in structured or unstructured form. Most of the time, we have to apply certain cleaning and transformation techniques in order to preprocess the text data before we use it. In this section, we are going to see some of those techniques to deal with text data, using TensorFlow.

Tokenization

The first technique to use on text data is known as tokenization. Tokens stand for individual words/symbols/numbers present in the text. For example, if we have a simple text, and we want to apply tokenization on it, we can simply create a tokenization instance and apply it, as shown following.

```
[In]: sample_text=['This is a chapter on text processing using
      tf','Text processing requires careful handling']
[In]: from tensorflow.keras.preprocessing.text import Tokenizer
[In]: tokenizer=Tokenizer()
[In]: tokenizer.fit_on_texts(sample_text)
```

The tokenizer collects all the distinct words appearing in the text and assigns a label to each one. It also assigns the labels in such a way that initial values are assigned to high-frequency tokens. We can validate this if we check the frequency of the words appearing in the sample. To view the labels of each token, we can call word_index on the tokenized text.

```
[In]: word_dict=tokenizer.word_index
[In]: print(word_dict)
[Out]:
{'text': 1, 'processing': 2, 'this': 3, 'is': 4, 'a': 5,
'chapter': 6, 'on': 7, 'using': 8, 'tf': 9, 'requires': 10,
'careful': 11, 'handling': 12}
```

Tokenizer does the heavy lifting in the background, by taking care of duplicate/similar words, removing punctuation, and converting letters to lower case. For example, if tf and tf! appear in the text, tokenization would consider both to be the same tokens, by removing the "!" in the background.

```
[In]: sample_edit_text=['This is a chapter on text processing
      using tf','Text processing requires careful handling','tf!']
[In]: tokenizer=Tokenizer()
[In]: tokenizer.fit_on_texts(sample_edit_text)

[In]: word_dict=tokenizer.word_index
[In]: print(word_dict)
[Out]:
 {'text': 1, 'processing': 2, 'tf': 3, 'this': 4, 'is': 5,
'a': 6, 'chapter': 7, 'on': 8, 'using': 9, 'requires': 10,
'careful': 11, 'handling': 12}
```

So far, we have seen labels assigned to each of these tokens, but at the end of the day, we are dealing with sentences, which are collections of words. Therefore, we must combine these individual labels in such a way as to represent entire sentences numerically. One of the most fundamental approaches to converting a sequence of words into numerical form is simply to apply text to sequence functionality on the entire text sentence.

```
[In]: seq=tokenizer.texts_to_sequences(sample_edit_text)

[In]: print(seq)
[Out]:

[[4, 5, 6, 7, 8, 1, 2, 9, 3], [1, 2, 10, 11, 12], [3]]
```

As we can see, we get three different arrays, representing individual sentences in the sample_edit_text. Although we are able to achieve our goal, there are still some gaps in this representation. One is that each array is of different length, which can be a potential problem when using these vectors in any sort of machine learning model training. To handle the different lengths of arrays, we can make use of something known as padding. This converts vectors of different lengths into vectors of the same length, by padding the vectors by a value of 0 at the beginning or end of a vector.

```
[In]: from tensorflow.keras.preprocessing.sequence import pad_
      sequences
[In]: padded_seq=pad_sequences(seq,padding='post')
[In]: print(padded_seq)
[Out]:
[[ 4  5  6  7  8  1  2  9  3]
 [ 1  2 10 11 12  0  0  0  0]
 [ 3  0  0  0  0  0  0  0  0]]
```

Now, we are left with three vectors, all of equal length.

Word Embeddings

We already saw the method to represent a set of words in a sentence in numerical form, using labels and the padding technique. There are some simpler and much more complicated methods, in addition to representing text in numerical form. We can basically divide them into two categories:

1. Frequency-based

2. Prediction-based

Frequency-based techniques include vectorizer, tf-idf, and hashing vectorizer, whereas prediction-based techniques involve such methods as CBOW (continuous bag-of-words) and Skip-Gram model. We will not go into the details of each of these methods, as there are enough articles and information related to these approaches available on various platforms. The idea of this section is to use word embeddings from our input data set and visualize them, using TensorFlow Projector. But before we jump into building a model, let's discuss briefly exactly what embeddings are.

Embeddings are, again, numerical representations of text information, but they are much more powerful and relevant, compared to other methods. Embeddings are nothing but the weights of the hidden layer of a shallow neural network that was trained on a certain set of text. We can decide on the size of these embeddings as per need (50, 100, or more) as well, but the key thing to remember here is that the embedding value can differ for the same text, based on different data it's been trained on. The core advantage that word embedding offers is that it captures the semantic meaning of the word, as it uses the idea of distributed representations. It predicts these embedding values, based on other words similar to that word. Therefore, there's an extent of dependence or similarity between a particular word and other similar words. We are going to see later in the chapter how similar words tend to have embeddings that are closer to each other in high-dimensional representation. There are some standard off-the-shelf methods available for calculating word embeddings, including the following:

> Word2Vec (by Google)
>
> GloVe (by Stanford)
>
> fastText (by Facebook)

Text Classification Using TensorFlow

In this section, we are going to build a deep neural network to predict the sentiment of a consumer review (positive or negative). The idea of building this network is not to focus on its accuracy but, rather, the process of dealing with text classification in TensorFlow 2.0 and the visualization of word embeddings. The data set that we are going to use for this task is the summary of people's review about the products on the Amazon web site. Instead of an entire review, we will use summary information. The data set is available with the code bundle for this book. We start by importing the required libraries and reading the data set.

```
[In]: import pandas as pd
[In]: import numpy as np
```

```
[In]: df=pd.read_csv('product_reviews_dataset.csv',encoding=
      "ISO-8859-1")
[In]: df.columns
[Out]: Index(['Sentiment', 'Summary'], dtype='object')
[In]: df.head(10)
[Out]:
```

	Sentiment	Summary
0	1	Good Quality Dog Food
1	0	Not As Advertised
2	1	"Delight" Says It All
3	0	Cough Medicine
4	1	Great Taffy
5	1	Nice Taffy
6	1	Great! Just As Good As the Expensive Brands!
7	1	Wonderful, Tasty Taffy
8	1	Yay Barley
9	1	Healthy Dog Food

```
[In]: df.Sentiment.value_counts()
[Out]:
1    486417
0     82037
```

As we can see, there are only two columns in the data frame (Sentiment, Summary), and we have positive counts on the higher side, compared to negative summaries (80K).

Text Processing

Now we apply a couple of text-cleaning techniques, using a helper function. In this helper function, we use a regular expression to remove unwanted symbols, characters, and numbers, to set the reviews into a standard format. We apply this helper function on the Summary column of the data frame.

```
[In]: import re
[In]: def clean_reviews(text):
          text=re.sub("[^a-zA-Z]"," ",str(text))
          return re.sub("^\d+\s|\s\d+\s|\s\d+$", " ", text)

[In]: df['Summary']=df.Summary.apply(clean_reviews)
[In]: df.head(10)
[Out]:
```

	Sentiment	Summary
0	1	Good Quality Dog Food
1	0	Not As Advertised
2	1	Delight Says It All
3	0	Cough Medicine
4	1	Great Taffy
5	1	Nice Taffy
6	1	Great Just As Good As the Expensive Brands
7	1	Wonderful Tasty Taffy
8	1	Yay Barley
9	1	Healthy Dog Food

As we can see, the text looks much cleaner now and ready for tokenization. Before tokenization, let's create the input and output columns from the data frame. As mentioned earlier, the goal of this exercise is not to achieve a very high accuracy but to understand the approach itself. Therefore, we are not going to split the data into Train and Test.

```
[In]: X=df.Summary
[In]: y=df.Sentiment
[In]: tokenizer=Tokenizer(num_words=10000, oov_token='xxxxxxx')
```

Here, by applying tokenizer, we are ensuring that we want to consider a maximum 10,000-word vocabulary. For unseen words, we use a default token.

```
[In]: tokenizer.fit_on_texts(X)
[In]: X_dict=tokenizer.word_index
[In]: len(X_dict)
[Out]: 32763
[In]: X_dict.items()
[Out]:
```

```
dict_items([('xxxxxxx', 1), ('great', 2), ('the', 3), ('good', 4), ('a', 5), ('for', 6), ('and', 7), ('not', 8), ('be
st', 9), ('it', 10), ('my', 11), ('love', 12), ('i', 13), ('but', 14), ('coffee', 15), ('this', 16), ('tea', 17), ('t
o', 18), ('of', 19), ('product', 20), ('is', 21), ('delicious', 22), ('taste', 23), ('s', 24), ('very', 25), ('in', 2
6), ('flavor', 27), ('dog', 28), ('like', 29), ('food', 30), ('excellent', 31), ('these', 32), ('t', 33), ('you', 3
4), ('tasty', 35), ('price', 36), ('yummy', 37), ('with', 38), ('as', 39), ('favorite', 40), ('ever', 41), ('too', 4
2), ('so', 43), ('stuff', 44), ('loves', 45), ('on', 46), ('snack', 47), ('are', 48), ('dogs', 49), ('better', 50),
('just', 51), ('healthy', 52), ('free', 53), ('no', 54), ('what', 55), ('cat', 56), ('awesome', 57), ('chocolate', 5
8), ('than', 59), ('them', 60), ('tastes', 61), ('nice', 62), ('yum', 63), ('one', 64), ('perfect', 65), ('at', 66),
('quality', 67), ('really', 68), ('sweet', 69), ('wonderful', 70), ('treat', 71), ('can', 72), ('all', 73), ('tastin
g', 74), ('bad', 75), ('chips', 76), ('cup', 77), ('buy', 78), ('your', 79), ('me', 80), ('treats', 81), ('have', 8
2), ('k', 83), ('hot', 84), ('cats', 85), ('be', 86), ('that', 87), ('from', 88), ('little', 89), ('amazing', 90),
('if', 91), ('they', 92), ('more', 93), ('sugar', 94), ('gluten', 95), ('cookies', 96), ('don', 97), ('easy', 98),
('organic', 99), ('much', 100), ('value', 101), ('mix', 102), ('green', 103), ('was', 104), ('way', 105), ('out', 10
6), ('ok', 107), ('fantastic', 108), ('only', 109), ('works', 110), ('pretty', 111), ('or', 112), ('ve', 113), ('sal
t', 114), ('amazon', 115), ('an', 116), ('up', 117), ('strong', 118), ('candy', 119), ('get', 120), ('drink', 121),
('our', 122), ('low', 123), ('water', 124), ('cereal', 125), ('happy', 126), ('made', 127), ('sauce', 128), ('deal',
129), ('popcorn', 130), ('cups', 131), ('oil', 132), ('real', 133), ('do', 134), ('fresh', 135), ('high', 136), ('wil
l', 137), ('eat', 138), ('go', 139), ('bars', 140), ('bar', 141), ('new', 142), ('had', 143), ('time', 144), ('ther
e', 145), ('coconut', 146), ('natural', 147), ('expensive', 148), ('baby', 149), ('worth', 150), ('find', 151), ('b
```

So, we have more than 32,000 unique words in the text. We now apply tokenization on entire sequences.

```
[In]: X_seq=tokenizer.texts_to_sequences(X)
[In]: X_seq[:10]
[Out]:
```

```
[[4, 67, 28, 30],
 [8, 39, 572],
 [531, 487, 10, 73],
 [1723, 1450],
 [2, 1486],
 [62, 1486],
 [2, 51, 39, 4, 39, 3, 148, 832],
 [70, 35, 1486],
 [1420, 2115],
 [52, 28, 30]]
```

As we can see, each summary gets converted into a vector, but of different lengths. We now apply padding (post), to make vectors of equal length (100).

```
[In]: X_padded_seq=pad_sequences(X_seq,padding='post',maxlen=100)
[In]: X_padded_seq[:3]
[Out]:
```

```
array([[   4,  67,  28,  30,   0,   0,   0,   0,   0,   0,   0,   0,   0,
          0,   0,   0,   0,   0,   0,   0,   0,   0,   0,   0,   0,   0,
          0,   0,   0,   0,   0,   0,   0,   0,   0,   0,   0,   0,   0,
          0,   0,   0,   0,   0,   0,   0,   0,   0,   0,   0,   0,   0,
          0,   0,   0,   0,   0,   0,   0,   0,   0,   0,   0,   0,   0,
          0,   0,   0,   0,   0,   0,   0,   0,   0,   0,   0,   0,   0,
          0,   0,   0,   0,   0,   0,   0,   0,   0,   0,   0,   0,   0,
          0,   0,   0,   0,   0,   0,   0,   0,   0],
       [   8,  39, 572,   0,   0,   0,   0,   0,   0,   0,   0,   0,   0,
          0,   0,   0,   0,   0,   0,   0,   0,   0,   0,   0,   0,   0,
          0,   0,   0,   0,   0,   0,   0,   0,   0,   0,   0,   0,   0,
          0,   0,   0,   0,   0,   0,   0,   0,   0,   0,   0,   0,   0,
          0,   0,   0,   0,   0,   0,   0,   0,   0,   0,   0,   0,   0,
          0,   0,   0,   0,   0,   0,   0,   0,   0,   0,   0,   0,   0,
          0,   0,   0,   0,   0,   0,   0,   0,   0,   0,   0,   0,   0,
          0,   0,   0,   0,   0,   0,   0,   0,   0],
       [ 531, 487,  10,  73,   0,   0,   0,   0,   0,   0,   0,   0,   0,
          0,   0,   0,   0,   0,   0,   0,   0,   0,   0,   0,   0,   0,
          0,   0,   0,   0,   0,   0,   0,   0,   0,   0,   0,   0,   0,
          0,   0,   0,   0,   0,   0,   0,   0,   0,   0,   0,   0,   0,
          0,   0,   0,   0,   0,   0,   0,   0,   0,   0,   0,   0,   0,
          0,   0,   0,   0,   0,   0,   0,   0,   0,   0,   0,   0,   0,
          0,   0,   0,   0,   0,   0,   0,   0,   0,   0,   0,   0,   0,
          0,   0,   0,   0,   0,   0,   0,   0,   0]], dtype=int32)
```

```
[In]: X_padded_seq.shape
[Out]: (568454, 100)
```

As a result of padding, we end up with a numerical representation (vector length of 100) for every summary in the data set. One last thing before we start building the model is to convert the target variable y from Panda's series object to a NumPy array.

```
[In]: type(y)
[Out]: pandas.core.series.Series
```

```
[In]: y = np.array(y)
[In]: y=y.flatten()
```

```
[In]: y.shape
[Out]: (568454,)
```

```
[In]: type(y)
[Out]: numpy.ndarray
```

Deep Learning Model

Now we can start building the deep learning model, which is going to be of sequential type. We are keeping the embedding size as 50, by declaring the output_dim as 50.

```
[In]: num_epochs = 10
[In]: text_model = tf.keras.Sequential([tf.keras.layers.
      Embedding(in put_length=100,input_dim=10000,output_dim=50),
    tf.keras.layers.Flatten(),
    tf.keras.layers.Dense(6, activation='relu'),
    tf.keras.layers.Dense(1, activation='sigmoid')
])
[In]: ext_model.compile(loss='binary_crossentropy',
      optimizer='adam',metrics=['accuracy'])
[In]: text_model.summary()

[Out]:

Model: "sequential_2"
```

Layer (type)	Output Shape	Param #
embedding_2 (Embedding)	(None, 100, 50)	500000
flatten_2 (Flatten)	(None, 5000)	0
dense_4 (Dense)	(None, 6)	30006
dense_5 (Dense)	(None, 1)	7

```
Total params: 530,013
Trainable params: 530,013
Non-trainable params: 0
```

We now train the model on the input data, by calling the fit method. At each epoch, we witness loss.

```
[In]: text_model.fit(X_padded_seq,y, epochs=num_epochs)
[Out]:
```

```
568454/568454 [==============================] - 60s 105us/sample - loss: 0.2218 - accuracy: 0.9098
Epoch 2/10
568454/568454 [==============================] - 60s 106us/sample - loss: 0.1889 - accuracy: 0.9248
Epoch 3/10
568454/568454 [==============================] - 60s 106us/sample - loss: 0.1721 - accuracy: 0.9327
Epoch 4/10
568454/568454 [==============================] - 60s 106us/sample - loss: 0.1578 - accuracy: 0.9387
Epoch 5/10
568454/568454 [==============================] - 335s 589us/sample - loss: 0.1482 - accuracy: 0.9425
Epoch 6/10
568454/568454 [==============================] - 62s 109us/sample - loss: 0.1414 - accuracy: 0.9455
Epoch 7/10
568454/568454 [==============================] - 59s 104us/sample - loss: 0.1357 - accuracy: 0.9480
Epoch 8/10
568454/568454 [==============================] - 58s 103us/sample - loss: 0.1311 - accuracy: 0.9499
Epoch 9/10
568454/568454 [==============================] - 60s 106us/sample - loss: 0.1272 - accuracy: 0.9517
Epoch 10/10
568454/568454 [==============================] - 59s 103us/sample - loss: 0.1234 - accuracy: 0.9533
```

Embeddings

Now that the model is trained, we can extract the embeddings from the model, using the layers function. Each embedding is a vector of size 50, and we have 10,000 embeddings, since our total words were set to 10,000.

```
[In]: embeddings = text_model.layers[0]
[In]: embeddings.weights
array([[-1.6631930e-03, -3.1805714e-03, -4.2120423e-03, ...,
         6.7197871e-03, -6.8611807e-05,  5.0362763e-03],
       [ 2.5697786e-02, -3.3429664e-01,  1.4324448e-01, ...,
         2.6591510e-01, -6.1628467e-01,  4.6738818e-01],
       [-1.2153953e+00, -5.7287562e-01,  1.3141894e+00, ...,
```

```
       1.6204183e+00, -8.5191649e-01,  9.6747494e-01],
      ...,
      [-4.6929422e-01, -7.9158318e-01,  1.0746287e+00, ...,
       1.3168679e+00, -8.7972450e-01,  7.3542255e-01],
      [-6.2262291e-01, -2.9126891e-01,  2.6975635e-01, ...,
       5.5762780e-01, -4.7142237e-01,  3.8534114e-01],
      [ 3.8236725e-01, -3.2562292e-01,  5.2412951e-01, ...,
       8.0270082e-02, -4.5245317e-01,  2.1783772e-01]],
      dtype=float32)>]
```

```
[In]: weights = embeddings.get_weights()[0]
[In]: print(weights.shape)
[Out]:(10000, 50)
```

In order to visualize the embeddings in the 3D space, we must reverse the key value for embeddings and respective words, so as to represent every word via its embedding. To do this, we create a helper function.

```
[In]: index_based_embedding = dict([(value, key) for (key,
      value) in X_dict.items()])

[In]: def decode_review(text):
    return ' '.join([index_based_embedding.get(i, '?') for i in text])

[In]: index_based_embedding[1]
[Out]:'xxxxxxx'
[In]: index_based_embedding[2]
[Out]:'great'

[In]:weights[1]
[Out]:
array([ 0.02569779, -0.33429664,  0.14324448,  0.08739081, 0.52831393,
        0.27268887,  0.07457237,  0.12381076,  0.10957576, 0.06356773,
       -0.5458272 , -0.3850583 , -0.61023813,  0.3267659 , -0.1641999 ,
```

```
        0.35547504,   0.16175786,  -0.29544404,  -0.29933476,  -0.4590062 ,
        0.31590942,   0.43237656,   0.32122514,   0.11494219,   0.05063607,
       -0.08631186,   0.42692658,   0.44402826,  -0.4839747 ,   0.2801508 ,
       -0.37493172,  -0.24629472,   0.11664449,   0.30983022,  -0.08926664,
        0.12418804,  -0.6622275 ,  -0.5364327 ,  -0.03189574,  -0.30058974,
       -0.22386044,  -0.46651962,   0.3162022 ,  -0.19460349,   0.10765371,
        0.46291786,  -0.15769395,   0.2659151 ,  -0.61628467,   0.46738818],
      dtype=float32)
```

In the final part of this exercise, we extract the embeddings value and put it into a .tsv file, along with another .tsv file that captures the words of the embedding.

```
[In]: vec = io.open('embedding_vectors_new.tsv', 'w',
      encoding='utf-8')
[In]: meta = io.open('metadata_new.tsv', 'w', encoding='utf-8')
[In]: for i in range(1, vocab_size):
          word = index_based_embedding[i]
          embedding_vec_values = weights[i]
          meta.write(word + "\n")
          vec.write('\t'.join([str(x) for x in embedding_vec_
          values]) + "\n")
meta.close()
vec.close()
```

TensorFlow Projector

Now that we have the individual embeddings and metadata for the data set, we can use TensorFlow Projector to visualize these embeddings in 3D space. In order to view the embeddings, we must first go to https://projector.tensorflow.org/, as shown in Figure 5-2.

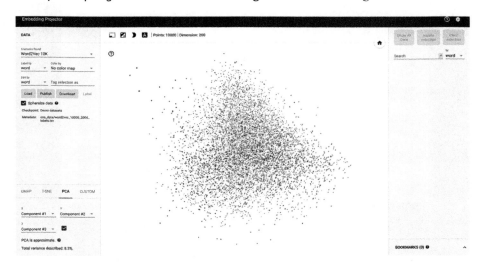

Figure 5-2. *TensorFlow Projector*

The next step is to upload the embeddings and metadata .tsv files that we saved in the last section, using the load option on the page, as shown in Figure 5-3.

123

Figure 5-3. *Embeddings data load*

Once loaded, the embeddings will become available in the projector, and we can observe the different clusters being formed, based on the values of each embedding, as shown in Figure 5-4.

Figure 5-4. *Embeddings visualization*

We can also observe that each embedding has a position in the overall context. Some are neutral, some are on the positive side, and some on the negative side of the center, as shown in Figure 5-5. We will now confirm if positive word embeddings are closer to each other in the visualization, and vice versa for negative words. Logically, the neutral words should be separate from both these clusters.

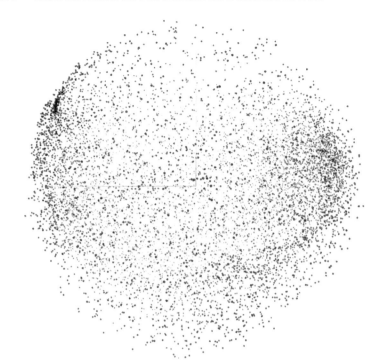

Figure 5-5. *Positive, negative, and neutral embeddings*

For example, if we look at the embedding of the word *like*, we can clearly see that similar words, such as *likeable*, *liked*, *likely*, and *likes*, are near to the actual like embedding, whereas opposite words, such as *dislike* and *disliked*, are at the other end of the group, as shown in Figure 5-6.

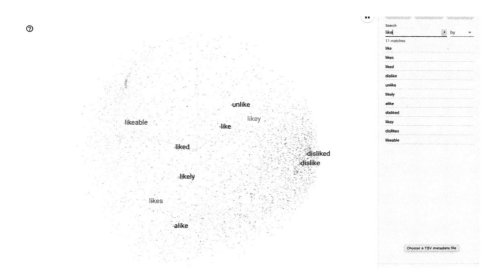

Figure 5-6. *Similar embeddings*

Let's consider one more example, to validate whether embeddings have captured the semantic meaning of the words. We take "fanta" as the root word with which to view the embeddings. We can clearly see that words such as *fantastic, fantabulous,* etc., are closer to each other, whereas a neutral word like *fantasy* is at the center, as shown in Figure 5-7.

127

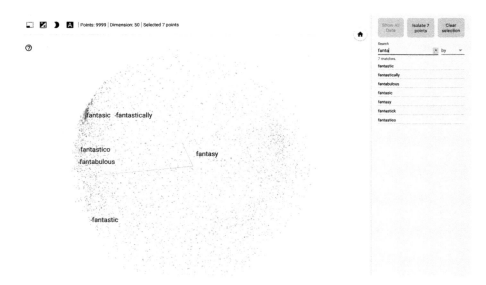

Figure 5-7. *Similar embeddings*

The final example demonstrates the actual distance separating embeddings from one another and which are the nearest embeddings. If we look at the word *worse* in the embedding projection, we see that the nearest similar words are *dangerous, lousy, poor, blah,* and *wasted,* as shown in Figure 5-8. These words also cluster at the negative end of the view.

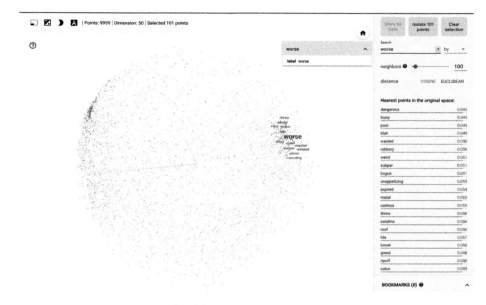

Figure 5-8. *Nearest embeddings*

Conclusion

This chapter provided a brief introduction to NLPs and the process of preprocessing text, using TensorFlow 2.0. We built a deep learning model to classify text sentiment and visualized the individual embeddings, using TensorFlow Projector.

CHAPTER 6

TensorFlow Models in Production

In this final chapter of the book, you will apply what you've learned in previous chapters and deploy the models built in TensorFlow 2.0 in a production environment. We believe that there are two principal aspects to using machine learning. The first is being able to build any sort of machine learning model and not integrate it with any application (standalone model). The other, more impactful aspect involves taking the trained machine learning model and embedding it with an application. The second approach is where things can become complicated, compared to the first, as we have to expose the trained model end points, in order for the applications to consume and use their predictions for activation or any other purpose. This chapter introduces some of the techniques by which we can deploy a machine learning model. We are not going to build a full-blown TensorFlow-based application. Rather, we will go over different frameworks to save a model, reload it for prediction, and deploy it. In the first part of the chapter, we review the internals of model deployment and their challenges. The second part demonstrates how to deploy a Python-based machine language model, using Flask (web framework). In the chapter's final section, we discuss the process of building a TensorFlow 2.0–based model.

© Pramod Singh, Avinash Manure 2020
P. Singh and A. Manure, *Learn TensorFlow 2.0*,
https://doi.org/10.1007/978-1-4842-5558-2_6

Model Deployment

The sad reality: the most common way Machine Learning gets deployed today is PowerPoint slides.

"Deploying Machine Learning at Scale," Algorithmia, `https://info.algorithmia.com/deploying-machine-learning-at-scale-1`, May 29, 2018.

According to a survey, less than 5% of commercial data science projects make it to production. For readers who have never undertaken any sort of software or machine learning deployment before, let us explain a few fundamental features of model deployment. It is more pertinent to the scalability aspect of an application, which can serve a bigger number of requests. For example, most anyone can cook at home for themselves or family members. On the other hand, it takes a different set of requirements, skills, and resources to successfully cook for a restaurant or online food service. The former can be done easily enough, whereas the latter might require a lot of planning, implementation, and testing before operating smoothly. Model deployment is similar. In scenarios in which a machine learning model has to be deployed within an application system, integration and maintenance become critical components. The successful deployment of a model takes a lot of planning and testing before an application platform matures to a level of self-sustaining prediction.

There is little doubt or argument regarding the fact that the true value of machine learning can only be unlocked or gained when it's deployed in an application or system. Without deployment, machine learning offers limited success and impact in today's business world. Deployment provides an exciting dimension to machine learning capability. Assuming that we have a fair understanding of a machine learning model, we can safely move on to its deployment aspect. To set the right expectations, let us make a bold statement at the outset. Machine learning is relatively easy compared to its deployment. The reason is that deployment brings a set of other parameters that must be taken into account, in order to build an end-to-end machine learning–based application, which is not always easy to carry out. Therefore, let's go over some of the challenges one might face while deploying a model into an application or system.

Isolation

Machine learning models can be built in isolation. In fact, all that we require to build a machine learning model is reasonably sized training data. However, deployment of a machine learning model doesn't work in isolation. Figure 6-1 (taken from Sculley et al., "Hidden Technical Debt in Machine Learning Systems," 2015) depicts the challenges that come with machine learning model deployment. In reality, a machine learning model code seems to be a very small component in the overall setup. It is the rest of the elements that demand consistent engagement and communication with the machine learning model.

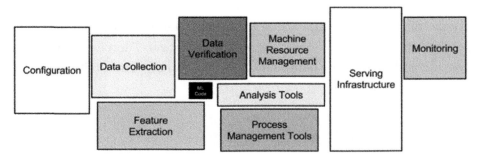

Figure 6-1. *Application management*

Collaboration

Most of us are aware that it's teams who build products or execute projects. Therefore, it takes a lot of collaboration and engagement to build or deploy a successful product. It's no different in the machine learning world, where

133

application developers might have to coordinate with data scientists, to deploy a model in a system. Issues arise, for example, when the model is built in one language, and DevOps or applications folks are using some other language.

Model Updates

Things around us hardly remain the same. However, a few things are changing so rapidly that technology has not been able to keep pace with the changing behaviors of users. Similarly, machine learning models must also be regularly updated, in order to remain relevant and highly efficient. This is easier to ensure with a standalone model, but it requires a lot of steps to update a model live in production.

Model Performance

The whole idea of using machine learning in applications is to be able to generalize well and help customers make suitable choices. This all depends on the performance underneath the model. Therefore, the tracking and monitoring of models in production become a critical part of the overall application.

Load Balancer

The final challenge in model deployment is the ability to handle requests at scale. Every application or platform should be designed in such a way that it can work seamlessly in high-traffic situations.

Now that we have reviewed the challenges faced in model deployment, we can go over some of the basic-to-intermediate steps to deploy Python-based models. Again, the focus of this chapter is to expose some of the available tools and techniques to deploy machine learning models, instead of building a full application.

Python-Based Model Deployment

There are multiple ways in which a machine learning model can be deployed in production. All depend on the requirement and load that is expected to be served by the model. In this section, we will go over a couple of approaches, to see how we can create, save, and restore a Python-based machine learning model for making predictions. We then move on to deploying TensorFlow-based models in production, in the last section.

Saving and Restoring a Machine Learning Model

At the end of the day, a machine learning model is simply a combination of a few scores, respective to every input feature used while training the model, which describes the relationship between given inputs and output in the best possible way. The ability to save any machine learning model (irrespective of being built in Python, R, or TensorFlow) allows us to use it later, at any point in time, for making predictions on new data, as well as to share it with other users. Saving any model is also known as serialization. This can also be done in different ways, as Python has its own way of persisting a model, known as *pickle*. Pickle can be used to serialize machine language models, as well as any other transformer. The other approach has the built-in functionality of sklearn, which allows saving and restoring of Python-based machine learning models. In this section, we will focus on using the `joblib` function to save and persist sklearn models. Once the model is saved on disk or at any other location, we can reload or restore it back, for making predictions on new data.

In the example below, we consider the standard data set for building a linear regression model. The input data has five input columns and one output column. All the variables are numeric in nature, so little feature engineering is required. Nevertheless, the idea here is not to focus on building a perfect model but to build a baseline model, save it, and then restore it. In the first step, we load the data and create input and output feature variables (X, y).

```
[In]: import pandas as pd
[In]: import numpy as np
[In]: from sklearn.linear_model import LinearRegression
[In]: df=pd.read_csv('Linear_regression_dataset.
      csv',header='infer')
[In]: df
[Out]:
```

	var_1	var_2	var_3	var_4	var_5	output
752	673	686	84	0.317	0.268	0.399
571	665	565	93	0.326	0.253	0.359
644	641	596	87	0.309	0.246	0.368
57	855	677	96	0.340	0.283	0.460
222	701	935	56	0.320	0.263	0.396
720	686	729	77	0.324	0.254	0.390
938	531	734	55	0.291	0.235	0.340
511	776	664	94	0.338	0.265	0.411
500	771	682	91	0.338	0.265	0.402
658	594	583	83	0.310	0.247	0.351

```
[In]: X=df.loc[:,df.columns !='output']
[In]: y=df['output']
```

The next step is to split the data into train and test sets. Then we build the linear regression model on the training data and access the coefficient values for all the input variables.

```
[In]: from sklearn.model_selection import train_test_split
[In]: X_train, X_test, y_train, y_test = train_test_split(X, y,
      test_size=0.25)
[In]: lr = LinearRegression().fit(X_train, y_train)

[In]: lr.coef_

[Out]: array([[ 3.40323422e-04,  5.78491342e-05,  2.24450972e-04,
         -6.65195539e-01,  5.01534474e-01]])
```

The performance of this baseline model seems reasonable, with an R-squared value of 87% on the training set and 85% on the test set.

```
[In]: model.score(X_train,y_train)
[Out]: 0.8735114024937244
[In]: model.score(X_test,y_test)
[Out]: 0.8551517840207584
```

Now that we have the trained model available, we can save it at any location or disk, using joblib or pickle. We name the exported model linear_regression_model.pkl.

```
[In]: import joblib
[In]: joblib.dump(lr,'linear_regression_model.pkl')
```

Now, we create a random input feature set and predict the output, using the trained model that we just saved.

```
[In]: test_data=[600,588,90,0.358,0.333]
[In]: pred_arr=np.array(test_data)
[In]: print(pred_arr)
[Out]: [6.00e+02 5.88e+02 9.00e+01 3.58e-01 3.33e-01]
[In]: preds=pred_arr.reshape(1,-1)
[In]: print(preds)
[Out]: [[6.00e+02 5.88e+02 9.00e+01 3.58e-01 3.33e-01]]
```

In order to predict the output with the same model, we first must import or load the saved model, using `joblib.load`. Once the model is loaded, we can simply use the `predict` function, to make the prediction on a new data point.

```
[In]: model=open("linear_regression_model.pkl","rb")
[In]: lr_model=joblib.load(model)
[In]: model_prediction=lr_model.predict(preds)
[In]: print(model_prediction)
[Out]: [0.36901871]
```

This was clearly done from a local disk space and not any cloud location, but to an extent, this approach would still work in production, as the pickled file of the model can be saved at a location in the production environment. For a couple of reasons, this is not the ideal way to deploy your model in production.

1. Limited access. Only users who have access to the production environment can use the machine learning model, as it is restricted to a particular environment.

2. Scalability. Having just a single instance of model prediction can result in serious challenges, once the load or demand for the output increases.

Deploying a Machine Learning Model As a REST Service

To overcome the limitations mentioned previously, we can deploy the model as a REST (representational state transfer) service, in order to expose it to external users. This allows them to use the model output or prediction without having to access the underlying model. In this section, we will make use of Flask to deploy the model as a REST service. Flask is

138

a lightweight web framework, built in Python, to deploy applications on a server. This book does not cover Flask in detail, but for those readers who have never used it, the following code snippet offers a brief introduction.

We create a simple .py file and write the subsequent lines of code, in order to run a simple Flask-based app. We first import Flask and create the Flask app. Then we decorate our main function, which is a simple Hello World!, with app.route, which gives the path for accessing the app (a simple /, in this case). The last step is to run the app, by calling the mains file.

```
[In]: pip install Flask
[In]: from flask import Flask

[In]: app = Flask(__name__)

[In]: @app.route("/")
[In]: def hello():
      return "Hello World!"

[In]: if __name__ == '__main__':
      app.run(debug=True)
```

We can now go to localhost:5000 and witness the Flask server running and showing "Hello World!"

Next, we are going to use the model that we built earlier and deploy it, using the Flask server. In order to do this, we must create a new folder (web_app) and save the model.pkl file. We are going to use the same model that we built in the preceding section. We can either move the model.pkl file manually to the web_app folder or re-save the model, using the earlier script in a new location, as shown following:

```
[In]: joblib.dump(lr,'web_app/linear_regression_model.pkl')
```

Let's begin to create the main app.py file, which will spin up the Flask server to run the app.

```
[In]: import pandas as pd
[In]: import numpy as np
[In]: import sklearn
[In]: import joblib
[In]: from flask import Flask,render_template,request
[In]: app=Flask(__name__)

[In]: @app.route('/')
[In]: def home():
            return render_template('home.html')

[In]: @app.route('/predict',methods=['GET','POST'])

[In]: def predict():
    if request.method =='POST':
            print(request.form.get('var_1'))
            print(request.form.get('var_2'))
            print(request.form.get('var_3'))
            print(request.form.get('var_4'))
            print(request.form.get('var_5'))
            try:
                    var_1=float(request.form['var_1'])
                    var_2=float(request.form['var_2'])
                    var_3=float(request.form['var_3'])
                    var_4=float(request.form['var_4'])
                    var_5=float(request.form['var_5'])
                    pred_args=[var_1,var_2,var_3,var_4,var_5]
                    pred_arr=np.array(pred_args)
                    preds=pred_arr.reshape(1,-1)
                    model=open("linear_regression_model.pkl","rb")
```

```
                  lr_model=joblib.load(model)
                  model_prediction=lr_model.predict(preds)
                model_prediction=round(float(model_prediction),2)
            except ValueError:
                  return "Please Enter valid values"
      return render_template('predict.html',prediction=model_
      prediction)
[In]: if __name__=='__main__':
                  app.run(host='0.0.0.0')
```

Let's go over the steps, in order to understand the details of the app. py file. First, we import all the required libraries from Python. Next, we create our first function, which is the home page that renders the HTML template to allow users to fill input values. The next function is to publish the predictions by the model on those input values provided by the user. We save the input values into five different variables coming from the user and create a list (pred_args). We then convert that into a numpy array. We reshape it into the desired form, to be able to make predictions in the same way. The next step is to load the trained model (linear_regression_ model.pkl) and make the predictions. We save the final output into a variable (model_prediction). We then publish these results via another HTML template (predict.html). If we run the main file (app.py) now in the terminal, we will see the page shown in Figure 6-2, asking the user to fill the values. The output is shown in Figure 6-3.

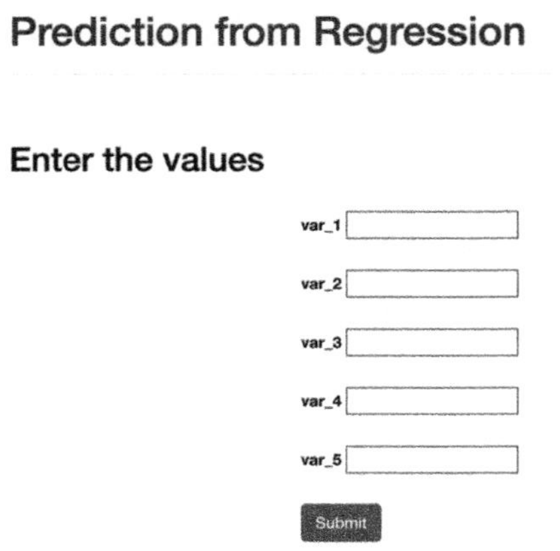

Prediction from Regression

Enter the values

var_1 [   ]

var_2 [   ]

var_3 [   ]

var_4 [   ]

var_5 [   ]

[Submit]

Figure 6-2. Inputs to the model

Prediction Result

3608.45

Figure 6-3. Prediction output

Templates

There are two web pages that we have to design, in order to post requests to the server and receive in return the response message, which is the prediction by the machine learning model for that particular request. Because this book doesn't focus on HTML, you can simply use these files as they are, without making any changes to them. But for curious readers, we are creating a form to request five values in five different variables. We are using a standard CSS template with very basic fields (Figure 6-4). Users with prior knowledge of HTML can feel free to redesign the home page per their requirements (Figure 6-5).

```html
<!DOCTYPE html>
<html>
<head>
    <<link rel="stylesheet" href="https://maxcdn.bootstrapcdn.com/
    bootstrap/3.3.7/css/bootstrap.min.css" integrity="
    sha384-BVYiiSIFeK1dGmJRAkycuHAHRg320mUcww7on3RYdg4Va+PmSTsz/K68vbdEjh4u"
    crossorigin="anonymous">

    <title>Prediction Using Flask</title>
    </head>

    <body>
        <h1><div style="text-align:centre"><font color='blue'>Prediction from
        Regression </font></div></h1>
        <hr>
        </br>

        <h2><div style="text-align:centre">Enter the values </div></h2>

        </br>

        <div class='container'>
            <div class='row'>
                <div class='col-6'>
                    <form method="POST" action="/predict">
                        <div class='form-group'>
                            <label for="var_1"><p class="font-weight-bold">
                            var_1</p></label>
                            <input type='text' name="var_1">
                            </div>

                            <div class='form-group'>
                                <label for="var_2"><p class="font-weight-bold">
                                var_2</p></label>
                                <input type='text' name="var_2">

                                </div>
                                <div class='form-group'>
                                    <label for="var_3"><p class="
                                    font-weight-bold">var_3</p></label>
                                    <input type='text' name="var_3">

                                    </div>
                                    <div class='form-group'>
                                        <label for="var_4"><p class="
                                        font-weight-bold">var_4</p></label>
                                        <input type='text' name="var_4">

                                        </div>
                                        <div class='form-group'>
                                            <label for="var_5"><p class="
                                            font-weight-bold">var_5</p></label>
                                            <input type='text' name="var_5">

                                            </div>

                                            <input class='btn btn-primary' type
                                            ='submit' value='Submit'>
                    </form>
                </div>
                </div>
                </div>

        </body>
</html>
```

Figure 6-4. *User input's HTML*

143

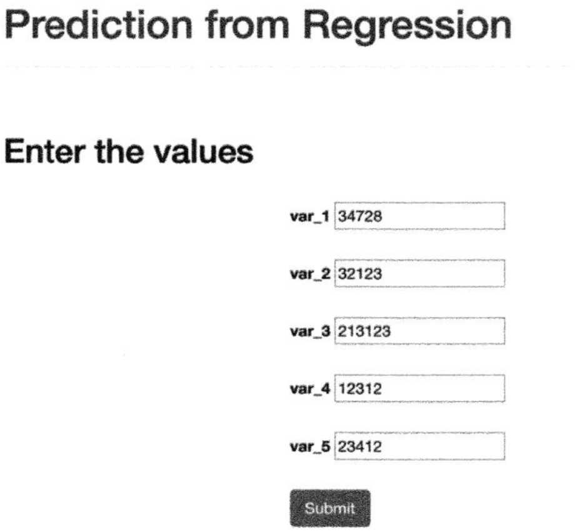

Prediction from Regression

Enter the values

var_1	34728
var_2	32123
var_3	213123
var_4	12312
var_5	23412

Submit

Figure 6-5. *Input web page*

The next template is to publish the model prediction back to the user (Figure 6-6). It is less complicated, compared to the first template, as there is just one value that we have to post back to the user (Figure 6-7).

```html
<!DOCTYPE html>
<html>
<head>
    <<link rel="stylesheet" href="https://maxcdn.bootstrapcdn.com/
    bootstrap/3.3.7/css/bootstrap.min.css" integrity="
    sha384-BVYiiSIFeK1dGmJRAkycuHAHRg320mUcww7on3RYdg4Va+PmSTsz/K68vbdEjh4u"
    crossorigin="anonymous">

    <title>Prediction by ML model</title>
    </head>

    <body>
        <h1><div style="text-align:center"><font color='blue'>Prediction
        Result </font></div></h1>
        <hr>
        <div class='card text-center' style="width:21.5em;margin:0 auto;">
            <div class="card-body">
                <p class="card text"><h1><font color='blue'>{{prediction}}</
                font></h1></p>
                </div>
                </div>
        </body>
</html>
```

Figure 6-6. *Model's output HTML*

144

Prediction Result

3608.45

Figure 6-7. *Model's output*

Now that we have seen how to deploy a model, using a web framework, we can move on to the last section of this chapter, which focuses on deploying a TensorFlow 2.0 model. There are two parts to this section. In the first, we will build a standard deep learning network, using tf.keras to classify images. Once the neural network is trained, we will save it and load it back, to make predictions on test data. In the second part of this section, we will go over the process to deploy the model, using the TensorFlow server platform.

Challenges of Using Flask

Although Flask is fine for deploying models as a service, it hits a roadblock when an application has numerous users. For a small-scale application, Flask can do a good job and manage the load. The alternative to Flask can be to use containers, such as Docker. For readers who have never used Docker, it is simply a technique to containerize the application, to run it irrespective of the platform. It resolves all the application dependency issues and runs much faster and easier, compared to a manual approach. Today, the common process to deploy any application in production is to containerize it, using Docker, and run it as a service on top of Kubernetes or any other cloud platform. One of challenges is to handle the number of requests made of the application. Therefore, Docker and Kubernetes can manage any number of increased requests, by managing via a built-in load balancer. This reduces the number of containers, if requests are fewer, and runs another instance of the applications, if load increases. In the next section, we are going to see how we can build a TensorFlow model and reload it for prediction in TensorFlow.

Building a Keras TensorFlow-Based Model

The data set that we are going to use to build this deep neural network is the standard Fashion-MNIST set we used previously. We start by importing the required libraries and ensuring that we have the latest version of TensorFlow.

```
[In]: import tensorflow as tf
[In]: tf.__version__
[Out]: '2.0.0-rc0'

[In]: from tensorflow import keras
[In]: import matplotlib.pyplot as plt
[In]: import numpy as np
[In]: from keras.preprocessing import image
```

The next step is to load the data set and divide it into training and test sets. We have 60,000 images in the training set on which we are going to train the network. Before training the model, we must execute a couple of steps.

1. Label the target classes, so as to recognize the image better.

2. Standardizing the size of each image.

```
[In]: df = keras.datasets.fashion_mnist
[In]: (X_train, y_train), (X_test, y_test) = df.load_data()
[In]: X_train.shape
[Out]: (60000, 28, 28)

[In]: y_train.shape
[Out]: (60000,)

[In]: labels=['T-shirts','Trouser','Pullover','Dress','Coat','S
       andal','Shirt','Sneaker','Bag','Ankle boot']
```

```
[In]: X_train=X_train[:50000]
[In]: X_val=X_train[50000:]

[In]: y_train=y_train[:50000]
[In]: y_val=y_train[50000:]

[In]: X_train=X_train/255
[In]: X_val=X_val/255
```

To see a sample image, we can use the imshow function and pass a particular image, as shown in a couple of examples following:

```
[In]: plt.imshow(X_train[100])
[Out]:
```

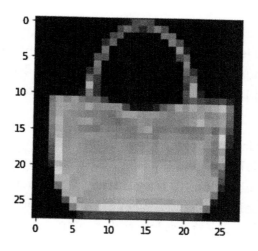

```
[In]: print(labels[y_train[100]])
[Out]: Bag

[In]: plt.imshow(X_train[1055])
[Out]:
```

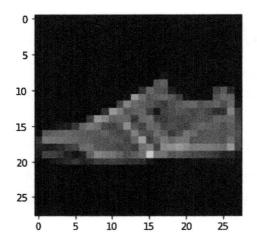

```
[In]: print(labels[y_train[1055]])
[Out]: Sneaker
```

The next step is to actually define and build the model. We use a conventional sequential model with three layers, the first containing 200 units, the second 100, and the last containing the prediction layer with 10 units of neurons.

```
[In]: keras_model = keras.models.Sequential()
[In]: keras_model.add(keras.layers.Flatten(input_shape=[28, 28]))
[In]: keras_model.add(keras.layers.Dense(200, activation="relu"))
[In]: keras_model.add(keras.layers.Dense(100, activation="relu"))
[In]: keras_model.add(keras.layers.Dense(10, activation="softmax"))

[In]: keras_model.compile(optimizer="sgd",loss=keras.losses.
      sparse_categorical_crossentropy,metrics=["accuracy"])
```

We now train the model on the training set and set the number of epochs to 10.

```
[In]: history = keras_model.fit(X_train, y_train,epochs=10)
[Out]:
```

```
Train on 50000 samples
Epoch 1/10
50000/50000 [==============================] - 2s 43us/sample - loss: 0.7453 - accuracy: 0.7543
Epoch 2/10
50000/50000 [==============================] - 2s 38us/sample - loss: 0.4983 - accuracy: 0.8275
Epoch 3/10
50000/50000 [==============================] - 2s 38us/sample - loss: 0.4528 - accuracy: 0.8419
Epoch 4/10
50000/50000 [==============================] - 2s 39us/sample - loss: 0.4243 - accuracy: 0.8501
Epoch 5/10
50000/50000 [==============================] - 2s 39us/sample - loss: 0.4055 - accuracy: 0.8565
Epoch 6/10
50000/50000 [==============================] - 2s 37us/sample - loss: 0.3887 - accuracy: 0.8631
Epoch 7/10
50000/50000 [==============================] - 2s 38us/sample - loss: 0.3755 - accuracy: 0.8679
Epoch 8/10
50000/50000 [==============================] - 2s 38us/sample - loss: 0.3649 - accuracy: 0.8716
Epoch 9/10
50000/50000 [==============================] - 2s 40us/sample - loss: 0.3530 - accuracy: 0.8746
Epoch 10/10
50000/50000 [==============================] - 2s 40us/sample - loss: 0.3444 - accuracy: 0.8774
```

Once the model is trained, we can test its accuracy on the test data. It appears to be close to 85%. We can definitely improve the model, by making changes in the network or using a CNN (convolutional neural network) that is more suitable for image classification, but the idea of this exercise is to save a model and call it later for predictions.

```
[In]: X_test=X_test/255
[In]: test_accuracy=keras_model.evaluate(X_test,y_test)
[Out]: 0.8498
```

Now, we save the model as a Keras model and load it back, using load_model for prediction.

```
[In]: keras_model.save("keras_model.h5")

[In]: loaded_model = keras.models.load_model("keras_model.h5")
```

In the following example, we load a test image (100), which is a dress, and then we will use our saved model to make a prediction about this image.

```
[In]: plt.imshow(X_test[100])
[In]: print(labels[y_test[100]])

[Out]:
```

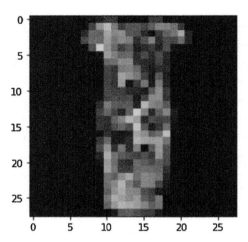

We create a new variable (new_image) and reshape it into the desired form for model prediction. The model correctly classifies the image as "Dress."

```
[In]: new_image= X_test[100]
[In]: new_image = image.img_to_array(new_image)
[In]: new_image = np.expand_dims(new_image, axis=0)

[In]: new_image = new_image.reshape(1,28,28)
[In]: prediction=labels[loaded_model.predict_classes(new_image)[0]]
[In]: print(prediction)
[Out]: Dress
```

One more example: We can select another image (500) and make a prediction using the saved model.

```
[In]: plt.imshow(X_test[500])
[In]: print(labels[y_test[500]])
[Out]:
```

Pullover

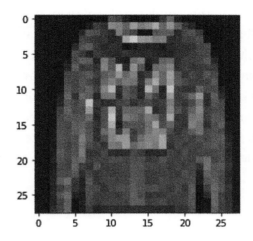

```
[In]: new_image= X_test[500]
[In]: new_image = image.img_to_array(new_image)
[In]: new_image = np.expand_dims(new_image, axis=0)

[In]: new_image = new_image.reshape(1,28,28)
[In]: prediction=labels[loaded_model.predict_classes(new_image)[0]]
[In]: print(prediction)
[Out]: Pullover
```

TF ind deployment

Another way of productionizing the machine learning model is to use the Kubeflow platform. Kubeflow is a native tool for managing and deploying machine learning models on Kubernetes. Because Kubernetes is beyond the scope of this book, we will not delve too deeply into its details. However, Kubernetes can be defined as a container orchestration platform that allows for the running, deployment, and management of containerized applications (machine learning models, in our case).

In this section, we will replicate the same model that we built previously and run it in the cloud (via Google Cloud Platform), using Kubeflow. We will also use the Kubeflow UI, to navigate and run Jupyter Notebook in the cloud. Because we are going to use Google Cloud Platform (GCP), we must have a Google account, so that we can avail ourselves of the free credits provided by Google for the use of GCP components. Go to `https://console.cloud.google.com/` and create a Google user account, if you do not have one already. You will be required to provide a few additional details, along with credit card information, as shown in Figure 6-8.

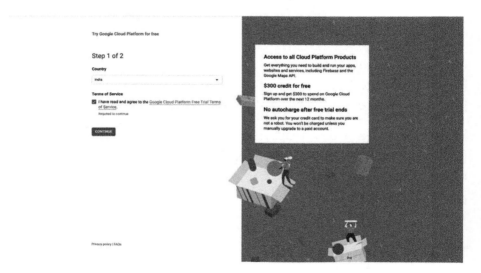

Figure 6-8. *Google user account*

Once we log in to the Google console, there are many options to explore, but first, we must enable the free credits provided by Google, in order to access the cloud services for free (up to $300). Next, we must create a new project or select one of the existing projects, for users already in possession of a Google account, as shown in Figure 6-9.

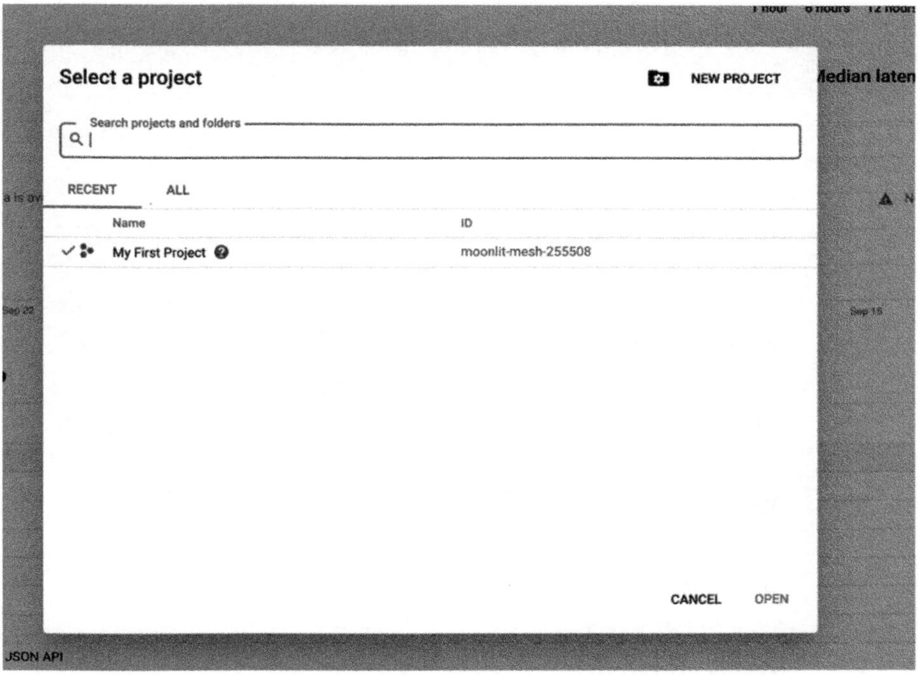

Figure 6-9. *Google project*

To use Kubeflow, the final step is to enable Kubernetes Engine APIs. In order to enable Kubernetes Engine APIs, we must go to the APIs & Services dashboard (Figure 6-10) and search for Kubernetes Engine API. Once this shows up in the library, we must enable it, as shown in Figure 6-11.

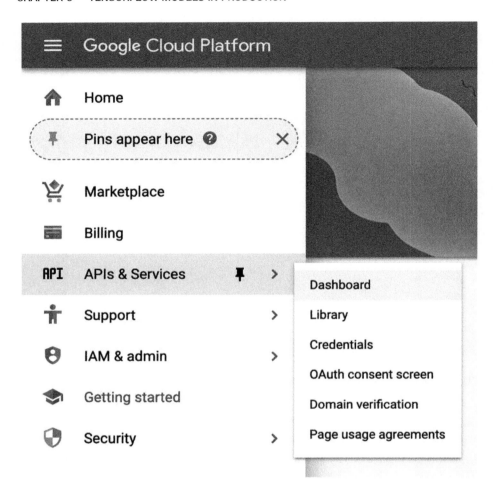

Figure 6-10. *APIs dashboard*

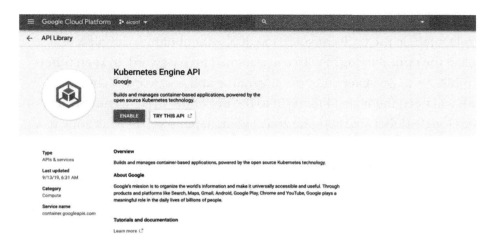

Figure 6-11. *Enabling Kubernetes APIs*

The next step is to deploy the Kubernetes cluster on GCP, using Kubeflow. There are multiple ways of doing this, but we are going to deploy the cluster by using a UI. Go to `https://deploy.kubeflow.cloud/#/` and provide the required details, as shown in Figure 6-12.

Figure 6-12. *Kubeflow deployment*

We must enter the project ID (to view the project details under the Project tab on the GCP console), the deployment name of choice, and select the option to log in with a username and password, to keep things simple. Next, we again enter our username and password of choice (we will need them again to log in to the Kubeflow UI). We can select the Google Kubernetes Engine zone again, depending on what zone is available, and choose Kubeflow version 0.62. Clicking Create Deployment ensures that all required resources will be up and running in about 30 minutes. We can also check if the Kubernetes cluster is up and running by going back to the Google console dashboard and selecting the Kubernetes Engine and Clusters option. It might take a few minutes before we can see a Kubernetes Engine cluster up and running. Now that the Kubeflow deployment is set up, we can simply click the Kubeflow Service Endpoint button, and a new UI page will be available. We must use the same username and password that we provided during the deployment phase, as shown in Figure 6-13.

Figure 6-13. *Kubeflow login*

Once we log in to the Kubeflow UI, we can see the Kubeflow dashboard, with its multiple options, such as Pipelines, Notebook Servers, etc., as shown in Figure 6-14.

Figure 6-14. *Kubeflow dashboard*

We must select Notebook Servers, to start a new notebook server. For a new notebook server, we must provide a few details regarding the desired configuration, as shown in Figure 6-15.

Figure 6-15. *Kubeflow Notebook Servers*

Now we must provide a few configuration details to spin up the server, such as base image (with pre-installed libraries and dependencies), the size of CPU/GPUs, and total memory (5 CPUs and 5GB memory suffices for our model). We can select the image with TensorFlow version 2.0, because we are building the model with that version. We must also add GCP credentials, in case we want to save the model to GCP's storage bucket and use it for serving purposes. After a while, the notebook server will be up and running, and we can click Connect, to open the Jupyter Notebook running on the Kubeflow server, as shown in Figure 6-16.

Figure 6-16. *Opening the Jupyter Notebook server from Notebook Servers*

Once Jupyter Notebook is up, we can select the option to create a new Python 3 notebook or simply go to its terminal and clone the required repo from Git, to download all the model files to this notebook. In our case, because we are building the model from scratch, we will create a new Python 3 notebook and replicate the same model built earlier in the chapter. It should work exactly as before, the only difference being that we are now using Kubeflow to build and serve the model. In case any library is not available, we can simply pip3 install the library and use it in this notebook.

Once the model is built and we have used the services of Kubeflow, we must terminate and delete all the resources, in order to avoid any extra cost. We must go back to the Google console and, under the Kubernetes clusters list, delete the Kubeflow server.

Conclusion

In this chapter, we explored the common challenges faced when taking machine learning models into production and how to overcome them. We also reviewed the process for saving a machine learning model (Python- and TensorFlow-based) and deploying it into production, using different frameworks.

Index

A

Artificial intelligence (AI), 1, 26, 54, 76

Artificial neural networks (ANNs), 55, 81, 97

B

Backward propagation, 58–61

Bagging technique, 48

Boosted trees method, 47
    ensemble methods, 48
        bagging technique, 48
        boosting technique, 49, 50
    gradient boosting, 49–52

Boosting technique, 49, 50

C

Colaboratory, 17–19

ConvNets, 75, *see* Convolutional neural networks (CNNs)

Convolutional neural networks (CNNs), 75
    architectures
        DenseNet, 93
        GoogleNet, 91

ResNet, 91, 92
        VGG-16, 89, 90
    convolutional layer
        definition, 77
        dot product, 78
        feature map, 79
        grayscale image, 78
        ReLU function, 79, 80
    fully connected layer, 81, 82
    pooling layers, 80, 81
    ReLU activation function, 86
    TensorFlow 2.0, 82–89

D, E

Databricks
    account and spin up, 19
    clusters, 20
    libraries options, 21
    notebook, 23
    PyPI source, 22
    TensorFlow package, 22

Deep neural network (DNN)
    hidden layers, 67
    Keras model, 71–74
    optimization function, 69
    output layers, 68

Printed by Printforce, the Netherlands